New York

BY THEME

DAY TRIPS

The State's Best Day Trips Outside New York City

Sandra Mardenfeld

Adventure Publications
Cambridge, Minnesota

Dedication

Dedicated to my family—here's to many more road trips—and the Greene family, who share our summer vacations, especially Debbie—the organizer of most of them.

Cover and book design by Jonathan Norberg
Front cover photo: Boldt Castle Power House, Alexandra Bay, NY: **JeniFoto/shutterstock.com**; map: **Globe Turner/shutterstock.com**

Back cover image: map: **boreala/shutterstock.com**

All photos by **Sandra Mardenfeld** except as noted on page pg. 144 (bottom): **Whitney Cranshaw, Colorado State University, Bugwood.org**; pg. 10: **James Dierks**; pg. 98: **Fly Creek Cider Mill & Orchard**; pg. 66: **Kadampa Meditation Center**; pg. 58: **Tom Nycz for Historic Hudson Valley**; pg. 49: **Wayne Peters**; pg. 126: **Fiona Shukri**; pg. 26: **The Wild Center**

This image is licensed under the Attribution-ShareAlike 4.0 International (CC BY-SA 4.0) license, which is available at https://creativecommons.org/licenses/by-sa/4.0/: pg. 65: **Adam Moss**

Photos used under license from Shutterstock.com: pg. 97: **Africa Studio**; pg. 143 (top): **John A. Anderson**; pg. 141 (map): **boreala**; pg. 142 (bottom): **Steve Byland**; pg. 148 (top): **Ozgur Coskun**; pg. 108: **Reid Dalland**; pg. 148 (middle): **Ethan Daniels**; pg. 136: **DJN Studios**; pg. 143 (bottom): **donatas1205**; pg. 149: **Dream79**; pg. 87: **fandangle**; pg. 145 (top): **Jeff Feverston**; pg. 20: **Fer Gregory**; pg. 142 (top): **Elliotte Rusty Harold**; pg. 145 (bottom): **HildeAnna**; pg 32: **Hsahtaw**; pg. 92: **Ritu Manoj Jethani**; pg. 81: **Wangkun Jia**; pg. 139: **J-photographe-videaste**; pg. 146 (top): **Breck P. Kent**; pg. 75: **Larry Knupp**; pg. 19: **Lisamcm48**; pg. 146 (bottom): **luca85**; pg. 9: **MasyaS**; pg. 16: **mervas**; pg. 88 and pg. 107: **Mihai_Andritoiu**; pg. 144 (top): **Christian Musat**; pg. 25: **Vasilchenko Nikita**; pg. 91: **Jam Norasett**; pg. 147 (bottom): **CJ Park**; pg. 39: **R. deBrujin Photography**; pg. 130: **Derek Robertson**; pg. 31: **Vadim Rodnev**; pg. 57: **Daniel M Silva**; pg. 15: **Fred Srgosso**; pg. 55: **Liz Van Steenburgh**; pg. 141 (bottom): **Svetocheck**; pg. 70: **sweens**; pg. 140: **toriru**; pg. 135: **Jonathan Vasata**; pg. 147 (top): **vilax**; pg 46: **VladG**; pg. 4: **Marian Wilson**; pg. 112: **Sara Yassin**; pg. 118 and pg. 122: **Colin D Young**; pg. 143 (middle): **Zamada**

New York Day Trips by Theme: The Best Day Trips Outside of the New York Metro Area
Copyright © 2020 by Sandra Mardenfeld
Published by Adventure Publications
An imprint of AdventureKEEN
330 Garfield Street South
Cambridge, Minnesota 55008
(800) 678-7006
www.adventurepublications.net
All rights reserved
Printed in China
ISBN 978-1-59193-893-4 (pbk.); ISBN 978-1-59193-894-1 (ebook)

Table of Contents

Hot-Air Ballooning, Lake George area

CHOOSE YOUR ADVENTURE: Do you love the water? You can float on a river by tube or raft, or ride the rapids—even dive into the St. Lawrence River to see shipwrecks from long ago. Like the view from up high? Try zip lining, hot-air ballooning, or heading up into the trees to tackle an aerial adventure course, full of obstacles to test your climbing and balancing skills.

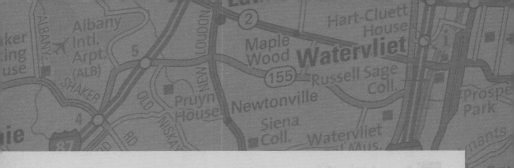

ADVENTURE

1 Dual Zip Line and Aerial Adventure Courses,

Peak Mountain Adventure Park at Peek'n Peak Resort
1405 Olde Road, Clymer NY 14724; 716-355-4141
www.pknpk.com

The Giant Dual Zipline is perfect for someone who doesn't like to adventure alone. You'll soar 40–50 feet off the ground and reach speeds of up to 30–50 mph on this 2,000-foot zip line—all while gazing at the surrounding mountains and valleys. Wanna go higher? The Soaring Eagle takes you 130 feet in the air with its 1,400-foot zip line that allows you to sit side by side with a friend. The park also has an Aerial Adventure Course (a 3-hour, self-guided experience that contains eight courses with 69 obstacles, including zip lines), Segway tours, biking, and miniature golf. Reservations advised. In the winter, there's tubing and skiing. The resort offers lodging, dining, a spa, and special events.

2 Float Trip/Tubing, Adirondack Adventure Center

877 Lake Ave., Lake Luzerne NY 12846; 518-696-6133
www.adktubing.com

Take a float trip—tubing will keep you cool and offer some startling scenery of the Adirondack Mountains. A guided Lazy River Tubing Adventure will take about 3 hours. Groups of 10 or more get a discount. Remember to tie your tubes together! Want more comfort than adventure? Rent deluxe tubes (with a backrest and cup holders), floating coolers, or cooler carriers (to make your own cooler river ready). If you want to control your speed more, you can take the same route by raft. The company also runs a treetop adventure course—with high-speed zip lines and an optional 63-foot free fall—and offers a discount for combo packages. Float tours run rain or shine; either way, you end up wet.

3 Hot-Air Ballooning, Lake George Area

Warren County Tourism Department, 1340 NY 9, Lake George, NY 12845; 800-95-VISIT
www.visitlakegeorge.com/recreation/air-adventures

See the Adirondack Mountains from a new view: in the air. Several vendors are available for all sorts of experiences—whether you want to catch your scenery by sunrise or sunset, privately or with a group, with champagne or snacks, or with photo ops. You'll float gently over historic villages, beautiful countryside, and Lake George—some flights even offer a glimpse of the Green Mountains in Vermont. Flights are available, weather permitting. The Adirondack Balloon Festival happens every fall in Queensbury, bringing together many varieties of hot-air balloons (think all colors and shapes), vendors, activities, a car show, and live music. The opening-day balloon launch has up to 20 hot-air balloons flying upward at the same time—with more added each day!

4 Jet Boating, Niagara Jet Adventures

555 Water St., Youngstown, NY 14174; 855-652-8687
www.niagarajet.com

See the Niagara River Gorge on a 32-foot, 1,650-horsepower boat that swiftly moves you through Class 5 whitewater rapids (appropriately named the Devil's Hole). These 60-minute guided tours, good for all ages over 4, feature 360-degree spins (dubbed the "Cowboy") at 60 mph. You will also learn about the gorge's history and see local sights like Fort Niagara and Brock's Monument. What you won't see is Niagara Falls—although you can stop by afterward since it's 15 minutes away. Be warned: sitting outside gets you wet enough that you'll need a change of clothes. The less adventurous can take a seat in the climate-controlled inside area and stay dry. Tours run as long as no ice is on the water.

5 Wreck Diving, Thousand Islands

1000 Islands International Tourism Council, 43373 Collins Landing Road,
Alexandria Bay, NY 13607; 800-847-5263
www.visit1000islands.com

The St. Lawrence River provides incredibly clear water and is
considered one of the best places for freshwater shipwreck diving.
The region has some two dozen wrecks in the area, including the
Islander, which suffered a fire in 1909 at its dock at Alexandria Bay
(located near the shoreline at Market Street—it's easily accessible
and has nearby parking). There are opportunities for beginner, intermediate, and experienced divers, and several vendors in Alexandria
Bay and Clayton can train and lead you on dives. You can also hire
charter boats. Generally, the diving season is from May to October,
when you'll find the most comfortable water temperatures. Don't
forget your underwater camera.

Alexandria Bay, NY

New York Museum of Transportation, Rochester

EARLY IN NEW YORK'S development, transportation became important as industry grew. While rivers and canals initially carried food and raw materials throughout the state, starting in the 1830s railroads connected cities and farms—allowing goods, information, and people to travel more easily. Automobile and airplane innovations followed. Glenn H. Curtiss, for instance, tested his planes—taking off from a frozen lake in Hammondsport—and helped make flying possible for more than just the birds.

AIRPLANES, RAILROADS, AND AUTOMOBILES

1 The Buffalo Transportation Pierce-Arrow Museum

263 Michigan Ave., Buffalo, NY 14203; 716-853-0084
www.pierce-arrow.com

The Pierce-Arrow Motor Company played a huge part in Buffalo's economic growth. Started in the 1870s as the George N. Pierce Company, it made household items such as birdcages. By 1908, the company had changed its name and was making luxury cars. The museum honors Buffalo's automotive history and the vehicle innovations Pierce-Arrow created. Besides many antique vehicles, the museum houses the Frank Lloyd Wright filling station, designed by the architect in 1927 but never built—the museum constructed it using the original plans as an installation in 2002 to complement its 80-plus bicycle, car, and motorcycle collection.

2 Champlain Valley Transportation Museum

12 Museum Way, Plattsburgh, NY 12903; 518-566-7575
www.cvtmuseum.com

A love of vehicles led a group of auto and history buffs to found this museum in 2000. But the museum offers more than just cars (although there are plenty of those); it looks at transportation's economic and social impact on the world as well as the region. A knowledgeable guide tells you about the cars, trucks, trains, motorcycles, and more on display and allows visitors to touch or board some of the collection. The museum specializes in Lozier vehicles—luxury cars once built in Plattsburgh. There's a fun model car room with more than 750 die-cast versions of autos, boats, trucks, and airplanes too.

3 Empire State Aerosciences Museum

250 Rudy Chase Dr., Glenville, NY 12302; 518-377-2191
www.esam.org

Housed in the Schenectady County Airport (you can literally fly to the museum), this site covers the aviation history of New York with interpretive exhibits, a restored aircraft collection, and an aviation library with more than 10,000 books and 5,000 photographs. Two buildings contain exhibits and displays on aviation pioneers, such as Amelia Earhart; World War I and II aircraft; as well as a thrilling flight simulator. The Agneta Airpark has over 20 restored historical aircraft, and you may sit in the cockpits of some of the military jet fighters. The museum offers a gift shop and organizes events, from film screenings to breakfast lectures on topics such as "So You Want to Become a Drone Pilot?"

4 Glenn H. Curtiss Aviation Museum

8419 NY 54, Hammondsport, NY 14840; 607-569-2160
www.glennhcurtissmuseum.org

Glenn Curtiss built bicycles and motorcycles before moving to aviation. The museum honors his days as an inventor and pilot, including a full-size replica of the *June Bug,* a flying machine Curtiss flew 5,000 feet in 1908 to win his first Scientific American trophy. The site offers a collection of motorcycles, bicycles, boats, automobiles, and 22 historic aircraft, along with exhibits on early aviation, the region's history, and local winemaking. There's a Restoration Shop where you can ask craftsmen questions while you watch them work on antique aircraft. The museum also has a 75-seat theater, special events (like motorcycle and car shows and Halloween activities), and a museum store.

5 Medina Railroad Museum

530 West Ave., Medina, NY 14103; 585-798-6106
www.medinarailroad.com

A great place for a train ride—you can enjoy the fall foliage, go for an autumn ride before attending a blues festival or spend some time with Santa and his reindeer. Best of all, the ticket price includes the museum, which has railroad exhibits, firefighter equipment, and a 204x14-foot model-train set, with multiple trains that wind through a variety of settings such as tiny farms, local towns, and big cities—and pass through tunnels and over bridges. The building, a former railroad depot, also has a gift shop that contains lots of railroad-oriented items, including toy trains, whistles, hats, and *Thomas the Tank Engine* and *Polar Express* products.

6 New York Museum of Transportation

6393 E. River Road, Rochester, NY 14586; 585-533-1113
www.nymtmuseum.org

There's lots to see at this museum, from historic vehicles to photo displays to an operating model railroad that has five trains and two trolleys. Trace transportation's progression, from horse to steam to the modern day, through interactive exhibits. You'll enjoy a 2-mile round-trip ride on an 87-year-old trolley car while gazing at the beautiful Genesee Valley area. Close your eyes and listen to the whistle and the click-clacks on the rail joints—it's like you're visiting the past (seasonal). Special trolley experiences are available, such as foliage and holly trolley rides (check the website for more information). There's also a research library and a gift shop. Open only on Sundays.

7 Old Rhinebeck Aerodrome

9 Norton Road, Red Hook, NY 12571; 845-752-3200
www.oldrhinebeck.org

At this working airfield in the Hudson Valley, you can see air shows (when scheduled) featuring historic airplane, and you can sometimes catch test flights and watch mechanics doing maintenance during the week. Biplane rides on a 1929 New Standard D-25 are by reservation only (weekdays and some weekends) and on a first-come, first-served basis (certain weekends only). The museum itself houses more than 60 vintage aircraft, lots of antique automobiles and motorcycles, and other memorabilia. There's also a gift shop, snack stand (be warned—cash only), and picnic area. The museum is open only from spring through fall, so double-check the website before going.

8 Rochester & Genesee Valley Railroad Museum

282 Rush Scottsville Road, Rush, NY 14543; 585-533-1431
www.rgvrrm.org

Want to go back in time? Enter this restored 1909 Erie Railroad passenger station and board a vintage train for a 1.5-mile round-trip journey through the museum's grounds. You can see a midcentury refrigerator car and a Lackawanna baggage car, as well as all types of trains, from diesel to steam locomotives. Exhibits about Rochester's industrial history and the trains that stopped at the depot are located at the beginning and end of your train ride. Get a behind-the-scenes peek at how the museum keeps its trains in working order at the Restoration Shop. There are also special-event trains where you can celebrate Oktoberfest, visit a pumpkin patch, see Santa Claus, and more. Open April–December.

1918 Curtiss JN4H "Jenny" at Old Rhinebeck Aerodrome

Adirondack chairs. Mirror Lake, Lake Placid, New York

THERE'S NOTHING LIKE the water during the summer—as
the saying goes, "Time wasted at the lake is time well spent."
When it's hot, you'll want to spend your time swimming, boating,
splashing, and playing around—and Lake George and Lake Placid
offer the scenic Adirondack Mountains as a backdrop for such
activities. When winter comes, these areas offer colder adventures, too, such as skating—and, in Lake Placid, dogsledding.

BEACHES AND LAKES

1 Lake George

Warren County Tourism, 1340 NY 9, Lake George, NY 12845; 800-95-VISIT
www.visitlakegeorge.com

This 32-mile stretch of water heaven offers lots of activities, from fishing to swimming to water sports. Definitely do one of the boat tours, with options for sightseeing, dinner, or sunset cruises—even theme nights such as Mardi Gras. The area has a rich history, and you'll hear tales about the Native Americans who once lived here; the French and Indian and Revolutionary Wars; and the rise of tourism in the area. Plus, there's the Fort William Henry Museum on the lake's south end, or you can take a drive on the 5.5-mile Prospect Mountain Veterans Memorial Highway with its 100-mile view from the mountain's summit. You'll find great shopping at the year-round factory outlets and lots of annual events, too, from the Lake George Music Festival to the Adirondack Nationals Car Show.

2 Lake Placid

Lake Placid Visitors Bureau, 2608 Main St., Lake Placid, NY 12946; 518-523-2445
www.lakeplacid.com

Visit many of the sites of the 1932 and 1980 Olympics—and when you tour the Olympic Sports Complex, consider taking a guided bobsled ride. An Olympic Passport allows access to all Olympic facilities and offers discounts. Lake Placid has more than 2,000 marked trails—with many hikers attempting to summit the 46 High Peaks in the Adirondack Mountains, all higher than 4,000 feet. The High Peaks also provide opportunities for rock climbing. The 128-acre, mile-long Mirror Lake provides stunning views and lots of activities—paddling alongside loons, swimming, fishing, or just lazing on Lake Placid Public Beach. In the winter, you can skate, dogsled, or take a toboggan from a 30-foot-high chute and travel 1,000 feet before hitting the lake's surface. There's also cross-country and backcountry skiing.

Darien Lake roller coaster

3 Six Flags Darien Lake

9993 Allegheny Road, Darien Center, NY 14040; 585-599-4641
www.darienlake.com

There's fun for all at Darien Lake—the website says it's New York's largest water and theme park, with rides like the Viper, a coaster with five inversions and a 70-foot drop. Besides the thrill rides, there's plenty of family-fun fare. The water park, Splashtown, offers several pools, a lazy river, rafting adventures, and speed slides, plus it has cabanas and private lounges for rent. There are concerts at the Darien Lake Performing Arts Center and events like the Harvest Festival. Stay the night at a variety of lodgings—including camping (cabin, tent, glamping, RV), guest houses, and a hotel—and enjoy select rides 30 minutes before everyone else. Darien Square provides shopping and dining opportunities, an arcade, and a laundromat. In the late spring and summer, fireworks decorate the skies every night.

Casino roulette

NEW YORK STATE has more than two dozen casinos and racinos—where you can watch and bet on races—with more than a dozen on reservations or tribal land operated by Native Americans. Some have a family-friendly vibe, with indoor pools and playground areas; others are more adult oriented. Casinos offer often more than just gambling, however; many are vacation destinations with luxurious resort hotels and restaurants.

CASINOS

1 Akwesasne Mohawk Casino

873 NY 37, Hogansburg, NY 13655; 877-992-2746
www.mohawkcasino.com

This casino has everything from slot machines to table games, poker, and bingo—even online gaming. Stay at the hotel or RV park, indulge at the spa (pay the conventional way or through points you earn with the Winners Club loyalty program), and laze in the indoor pool or hot tub. More than half a dozen places for dining include a buffet, sports bar, steak house, and food court. Every day there's some sort of promotion or special event like contests, giveaways, tournaments, and drawings (see promotions calendar). Several packages are available, including one that offers two tickets to the Akwesasne Cultural Center, 3 miles away. Wondering what to pack when you go? Check out the casino's weather camera on its website.

2 Del Lago Resort & Casino

1133 NY 414, Waterloo, NY 13165; 855-335-5246
www.dellagoresort.com

Located in the beautiful Finger Lakes region, this casino has more than 1,000 slots and 60 table games, including poker. Whether you stay at the hotel or not, you can visit their spa, which has a wonderful steam room, sauna, sanctuary space, fitness center, wellness classes, even lunch (where you can imbibe on local alcoholic beverages). Several packages are available; check the website. Dining options include a buffet and food court as well as *Top Chef* contestant Fabio Viviani's Portico. You can enjoy entertainment at the Vine Theater and throughout the resort, from comedians to Chippendales dancers to weekend DJs to all types of bands and musicians.

3 Resorts World Catskills Casino

888 Resorts World Dr., Monticello, NY 12701; 833-586-9358
www.rwcatskills.com

The numbers say it all: about 150 live table games, 1,600 slot machines, 19 tables of poker—all that and a view of the Catskills Mountains. The 100,000-square-foot casino also offers lots of dining

Casinos

options, from a 24/7 bistro to celebrity chef Scott Conant's Italian-inspired steak house to Mexican and Asian options. The Crystal Life Spa offers an assortment of holistic therapies, including their unique Spa Wave Bed Experience that provides 30 minutes of sound therapy treatment with the option of a moisturizing wrap or reflexology. Two hotels provide accommodations—check out some of the interesting packages, pairing your hotel room with an adventure like an off-road trip, a go-kart excursion, or a show at Bethel Woods.

4 Tioga Downs Casino

2384 W. River Road, Nichols, NY 13812; 888-946-8464
www.tiogadowns.com

This casino offers more than traditional gaming and slots: there's much to do besides gambling (although there are about 890 slot machines, 28 table games, and six poker tables—and more in the high-limits room). The site hosts rock and country concerts, antiques markets, trivia nights, and bands. A half dozen dining options await, from a buffet to a sports bar to a barbecue joint. The 5/8-mile Tioga Downs Casino harness racetrack, part of the old Tioga Park, features some of the top races in the country, such as the $300,000 Cane Pace. You can enjoy live races from May to September and yearlong simulcasting. There's also a golf club and a hotel.

5 Turning Stone

5218 Patrick Road, Verona, NY 13478; 800-771-7711
www.turningstone.com

Part resort, part casino, Turning Stone provides 3,400 acres of fun, gambling, fine dining, and sports. Golfers will find several courses—such as the 18-hole Atunyote, Kaluhyat, and Shenendoah, which offer PGA-level golf in beautiful, natural settings and a golf academy. There's also the Golf Dome, with driving ranges, an indoor practice area, simulators—and a store. Tennis fans can play in the climate-controlled Sportsplex or outdoors. There's racquetball, deer hunting on a 3,000-acre preserve, and fishing on the Salmon River. There are also four hotels and an RV park, two spas, a fitness club, more than 15 restaurants, and entertainment like pro boxing, concerts, and theater. Finally, there's also a 125,000-square-foot gaming floor that rivals that of a Las Vegas casino.

6 Vernon Downs

4229 Stuhlman Road, Vernon, NY 13476; 877-888-3766
www.vernondowns.com

The hotel and adjoining casino offer over 500 gaming machines and nearby horse racing at a track that has hosted events like the Empire Breeders Classic. A good place for kids, Vernon Downs has an indoor heated pool, an arcade in the hotel, and a play area and bounce house during racing season at the track (April–November). More than a half dozen dining options range from buffets to a sports bar to casual restaurants. Other features include daily simulcasting, self-bet terminals for racing, and lottery scratch-off machines. Performers such as Joan Jett have played at the casino, and every Thursday night there is an open mic where local musicians appear (see events calendar). Newcomers should join the Player's Club to receive free play time.

Casinos

Ace, king and poker chips stack

Wild Walk, The Wild Center

WHEN IT'S FAMILY TIME, you want to strengthen your relationships by making memories that last—and it's even better when activities involve learning and fun. All of these places offer original experiences that teach about different lifestyles (the Amish Trail), natural phenomena (*Maid of the Mist*), and the beauty of animals (all the rest!). Enjoy exploring New York together.

FAMILY FUN

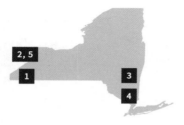

1 Amish Trail, Cattaraugus County/ Chautauqua-Allegheny

Amish Trail Welcome Center, Randolph Area Municipal Building, 72 Main St., Randolph, NY 14772; 716-358-9701
www.amishtrail.com

The Amish, who value faith and community and live without modern conveniences such as electricity or cars, settled in Cattaraugus County in the Enchanted Mountains (with some also in the Chautauqua-Allegheny region). Along the Amish Trail are many businesses that the Amish run from their homes or a nearby building that you can visit. You'll find all kinds of homemade goods, such as jams, produce, quilts, and toys. Businesses are closed on Sundays and holidays; look for OPEN signs in the front yards. Along these roads, you'll see the Amish in their plain dress, riding in horse-drawn buggies and tending to their farms—do not take photos of them, though, since it's against their beliefs. Get an interactive map online, or go to the Welcome Center for a brochure.

2 Aquarium of Niagara

701 Whirlpool St., Niagara Falls, NY 14301; 716-285-3575
www.aquariumofniagara.org

Through expert talks, animal feedings, sea lion shows, and exhibits, you'll learn about aquatic life. You'll get to meet the many harbor seals the aquarium rescues, rehabilitates, and releases. There's also the Humboldt penguins display, where you'll hear about the aquarium's conservation efforts, and many tanks of fish and invertebrates—such as sharks, eels, octopuses, seahorses, piranhas, and turtles—for you to see. Get a behind-the-scenes perspective with a penguin or seal encounter, and watch their care and training up close. You can also become a trainer for the day, spending time with a marine-animal professional, seals, and sea lions, or helping prepare fish for their meals (book all encounters online for an extra fee). Special events are also held; see the website for information on beach cleanups and sensory-friendly nights.

3 Bailiwick Animal Park & Riding Stables

118 Castle Road, Catskill, NY 12414; 518-678-5665
www.bailiwickranch.com

Come for the animals, stay for the activities. The animal park has exotic and domestic creatures, so you'll see not only tigers, llamas, and alligators but also pigs and sheep. The Bailiwick, a Scottish-style castle, is the home of the Koschitzki family, who started a horseback-riding business on the site in 1963; still in operation, it offers riding lessons and trail rides. The 4-acre animal park, opened in 2007, contains more than 40 exhibits, a petting zoo and feeding area, and a playground and picnic area (open April–November). The adrenaline driven will appreciate the 5-acre Paintball Park. There's also cowboy-style camping where you stay in covered wagons that feature four bunk beds and an outdoor fire pit, picnic table, and grill (a more primitive lean-to is also available).

4 Bear Mountain Trailside Museums & Zoo

55 Hessian Dr., Bear Mountain, NY 10911; 845-786-2701
www.trailsidezoo.org

The Trailside Museums & Zoo is in the Bear Mountain State Park, about a 20-minute walk from the parking lots. You'll find wildlife (black bear, coyote, red fox, birds), four museums (Herpetology House, Nature Study, Geology, History), and an amphitheater where educational programs and concerts are held. There's also a butterfly garden and a trail that leads to Fort Montgomery, a military post during the Revolutionary War. You will also see well-worn backpackers: Trailside is part of the 2,200-mile Appalachian Trail (extending from Georgia to Maine), which winds through the shady zoo, dotted with benches. Picnicking is not allowed at Trailside, but there's plenty of space for it elsewhere in the park, which also has (depending on the season) boating rentals on Hessian Lake, hiking trails, a merry-go-round, an ice rink, and a pool.

5 *Maid of the Mist*

1 Prospect St., Niagara Falls, NY 14303; 716-284-8897
www.maidofthemist.com

The first *Maid of the Mist*—initially a steamboat—was built in 1846 to carry people and cargo across the Niagara River. When a suspension bridge took away its need, the boat began ferrying sightseers. Today, getting close to the thundering falls is still big business, with more than 1.6 million tourists taking in the view as water rains down on their poncho-clad forms. Even the famous enjoy the spectacle, with actor Hugh Jackman, singer Mick Jagger, and former president Jimmy Carter just some of the luminaries who have enjoyed the boat ride past

the American falls into the basin of Horseshoe Falls. Departures are every 15 minutes, and tours last for about 20 minutes. The hooded rain poncho is yours to keep as a souvenir (seasonal).

6 The Wild Center

45 Museum Dr., Tupper Lake, NY 12986; 518-359-7800
www.wildcenter.org

Celebrate the history and environment of the Adirondacks with interactive exhibits. The museum encourages tactile experiences: in the Naturalists Cabinet, for instance, you can open boxes of bones. The floor-to-ceiling windows of the facility bring nature indoors as you gaze at the pond that laps against the building. Stroll along the Living River Trail to see the 2,000 live creatures that inhabit local lakes, bogs, streams, and rivers. At Otter Falls, view the playful exploits of the animals. Outside the 115-acre grounds are three trails. Wild Walk transforms the forest into a path across the treetops with swinging bridges, a four-story treehouse, and a human-size spiderweb suspended 24 feet off the ground. iForest, an immersive sound experience, takes you through the woods while a choral work alternates with spoken-word pieces from 24 speakers hidden in the trees.

7 Woodstock Sanctuary

2 Rescue Road, High Falls, NY 12440; 845-247-5700
www.woodstocksanctuary.org

This nonprofit that houses nearly 400 rescued animals (like Caesar the cow, from a squalid petting zoo) offers weekend tours, lasting about 1 hour. You'll walk about a mile and a half as you meet all the residents in their respective settings, whether that's yards, barns, or pastures. The guide will tell you all of the creatures' stories—where they were initially, the details of the rescue, and the frank realities of what would have happened to them if the sanctuary did not exist. The Visitor's Center serves vegan snacks, and on-site accommodations are available on select days in the Grey Barn (which has five bedrooms each with an en suite bathroom and terrace; vegan breakfast and private tour included). Open Saturdays and Sundays only, from April through October.

Tourists in front of Niagara's Bridal Veil Falls

Buffalo & Erie County Botanical Gardens

"A GARDEN TO walk in and immensity to dream in—what more could he ask? A few flowers at his feet and above him the stars," said *Les Misérables* author Victor Hugo. Forty years of research have shown that green spaces make people healthier and happier, according to *Parks & Recreation* magazine. So go visit a garden and release some stress.

GARDENS AND ARBORETUMS

1 Buffalo & Erie County Botanical Gardens, *Buffalo*. *34*
For more than 100 years, these gardens have awed visitors with their beautiful
conservatory and their exotic and native plants and flowers.

2 Cornell Botanic Gardens, *Ithaca* *34*
Adjacent to Cornell University, this site includes a 100-acre arboretum, various
gardens, and natural areas with trails and gorges.

3 Highland Park, *Rochester* *35*
Glacial deposits created the hills and valleys that Highland Park sits on. It features
some 1,200 lilac shrubs, a conservatory, and a castle.

4 Innisfree Garden, *Millbrook*. *35*
The 150-acre Chinese-style site is one of the "world's 10 best gardens," according
to its website, with waterfalls, rocks, terraces, and greenery.

5 Landis Arboretum, *Esperance* *35*
Overlooking the Schoharie Valley, this public garden features lovely views and an
arboretum, plus workshops and arts and crafts.

6 Mohonk Mountain House, *New Paltz* *36*
The resort offers many things, from activities to dining to gardens. Each year, its
Victorian Show Garden offers a new theme.

7 Montgomery Place, *Annandale-on-Hudson*. *36*
You will find woodland trails, flower and herb gardens, orchards, and a mansion
on this 380-acre property.

8 Mountain Top Arboretum, *Tannersville*. *37*
A museum of trees and shrubs located in the Catskill Mountains takes you 2,400
feet for spectacular views and learning opportunities.

9 Sonnenberg Gardens & Mansion State Historic Park,
Canandaigua *37*
This 50-acre estate, located in the Finger Lakes region, features flower gardens,
greenhouses, and a mansion that you can tour.

10 Yaddo Gardens, *Saratoga Springs* *38*
This historic artists' retreat on 400 acres in Saratoga contains a rose garden and
a woodland rock garden, both free to the public.

1 Buffalo & Erie County Botanical Gardens

2655 South Park Ave., Buffalo, NY 14218; 716-827-1584
www.buffalogardens.com

Initially called the South Park Conservatory, designed by Lord & Burnham (famous designers of Victorian glass houses), the site opened in 1900. Its look was based on England's iconic Crystal Palace, which was destroyed in a 1936 fire. Six more greenhouses were built in 1907, and the conservatory's name changed in 1981. Today, the greenhouses offer exotic environments to explore like the Florida Everglades, Panama, and Southeast Asia, as well as exhibits on carnivorous and medicinal plants. There's also a multitude of gardens and exhibits. For kids, there's a Family Garden with a sandbox, toys like miniature lawn mowers, and interactive stations. Don't miss the Outdoor Children's Garden. The Archangel Gallery displays photography or artwork on topics such as the Botanical Gardens, nature, or Buffalo. The site also offers events and classes.

2 Cornell Botanic Gardens

Nevin Welcome Center, 124 Comstock Knoll Dr., Ithaca, NY 14850; 607-255-2400
www.cornellbotanicgardens.org

Associated with the beautiful Cornell University campus, these gardens provide teaching opportunities for students and visitors—and the gardens are free and open every day year-round. Start your visit at the Welcome Center, where you can see interpretive exhibits and art displays. The 100-acre F. R. Newman Arboretum lets you see the diversity of trees and shrubs as you learn about native and other species. You'll see nine types of trees alone, from dogwood to maples to oak. You'll also encounter specialty plots like the shady Treman Woodland Walk, with a streamside garden. A Sculpture Garden features 10-ton concrete monolith-like structures created in 1961 by architecture students, way before there was an arboretum. You can also see 11 natural areas on the campus, including the Cascadilla Gorge Trail, which connects Cornell with downtown Ithaca.

3 Highland Park

450 Highland Ave., Rochester, NY 14620; 585-256-4950
www.cityofrochester.gov/highlandpark

Famous landscape architect Frederick Law Olmsted wanted the place-
ment of trees, flowers, and shrubs to seem natural in this park, even
though everything was planned and planted appropriately. There are
quite a variety of plants, from 1,200 lilac shrubs to a rock garden with
dwarf evergreens to 35 types of magnolias—as well as a collection of
Japanese maples, 700 types of rhododendrons, and lots of pansies that
bloom in a design that changes yearly. At the park, you can explore
hiking paths; a Vietnam Memorial; the Lamberton Conservatory, with
exhibits that change five times a year; the historic Warner Castle,
which offers several gardens itself (including a cool sunken one); and
the John Dunbar Memorial Pavilion, which has an outdoor amphitheater used for concerts and films. Picnic areas are available.

4 Innisfree Garden

362 Tyrrel Road, Millbrook, NY 12545; 845-677-8000
www.innisfreegarden.org

Named for a Yeats poem, this 150-acre garden took decades to create.
Artist/teacher Walter Beck and gardener/heiress Marion Burt Beck initially wanted English-style grounds that would match their home. But
the land dictated something else, and Walter created several Chinese
cup gardens, a term he coined to describe the asymmetrical sections of
greenery, rocks, flowers, and waterways that he developed. Landscape
architect Lester Collins started working with the Becks in 1938, linking
the individual gardens together using traditional Chinese and Japanese
design principles. Today the garden has multiple paths that you can
meander through. Visitors can navigate the garden on their own or
book a private guided tour. It's a contemplative place, so see it alone
or with friends who will respect the ambience. Events include lectures,
walks, and tours (see calendar). Open Wednesdays–Sundays in season.

5 Landis Arboretum

174 Lape Road, Esperance, NY 12066; 518-875-6935
www.landisarboretum.org

An arboretum and public garden in one, it spans more than 200 acres
in both Schoharie and Montgomery Counties. Forty acres are devoted
to trees, shrubs, and perennials through the arboretum, including
oaks, conifers, and two old-growth forests. There are both native and
international plant varieties. The rest of the space contains natural
areas, woodlands, wetlands, fields, and over 14 miles of trails (maps

are available in the Welcome Center). There are also some oversize sculptures in the fields by artist Samuel E. Bates—like the Landisaurus, a skeletal dinosaur near the pond by the barn. Leashed dogs are welcome except during plant sales (spring and fall) and the Forest 5K (a yearly run . . . or walk). For bird-watchers, the arboretum has nesting boxes throughout. Picnic tables are available.

6 Mohonk Mountain House

1000 Mountain Rest Road, New Paltz, NY 12561; 855-883-3798
www.mohonk.com

Mohonk Mountain House is known for many things: a historic castle-like hotel; all types of activities; a luxurious spa and pool; sumptuous meals; nightly entertainment; and access to hiking, boating, and a variety of outdoor sports. Then there are the gardens. When Albert Smiley purchased the space in 1870, he spent some 10 years installing elaborate gardens. Today, you'll find a multitude of flowers and greenery, including rose and herb gardens. The annual Victorian Show Garden features a new theme every year, using more than 300 types of flowers and plants to create it. The Mohonk Greenhouse grows many of these, and it and the Garden Shop are open to visitors. For kids, there is also a Victorian maze and a children's garden. Day and overnight guest packages are available.

7 Montgomery Place

25 Gardener Way, Annandale-on-Hudson, NY 12504; 845-752-5000
www.bard.edu/montgomeryplace

The 380-acre property, adjacent to Bard College, once belonged to Janet Livingston, the wife of Revolutionary War General Richard Montgomery, who died during the Battle of Quebec. A designated National Historic Landmark, the mansion is open for tours on Saturdays from June through October. Livingston had the mansion built in the federal style, but 19th-century architect A.J. Davis redesigned it, and the home is considered his finest neoclassical country house, according to the website. The grounds are open daily and include woodland trails (both the Sawkill and South Woods Trails are uneven and sometimes muddy, so choose appropriate footwear), a farm, flower and herb gardens, and several other buildings as well as an orchard. Programs and exhibitions are held on the estate, including outdoor yoga and concerts.

8 Mountain Top Arboretum

4 Maude Adams Road, Tannersville, NY 12485; 518-589-3903
www.mtarboretum.org

This public garden in the Catskill Mountains takes you up 2,400 feet and offers trails and boardwalks through 178 acres of meadows, wetlands, forest, and bedrock. It was founded by Dr. Peter Ahrens and his wife, Bonnie, who wanted to study how the winter impacted various native and exotic trees. They then created the arboretum in 1977 with their original 7-acre test site. Now the area provides opportunities to study horticulture and also offers hiking, birding, and snowshoeing. There are four main paths to see, and you should allocate about 30–45 minutes for each. Families will want to try the Woodland Walk, which has easy trails, a fairy garden, and a boulder amphitheater. The arboretum also offers lectures, workshops, and other programming. Note that no picnicking is allowed on the trails.

9 Sonnenberg Gardens & Mansion State Historic Park

151 Charlotte St., Canandaigua, NY 14424; 585-394-4922
www.sonnenberg.org

This country estate from the Victorian era sits on 50 acres. You can explore the Lord & Burnham greenhouse and a variety of gardens (including Italian, Japanese, and rose gardens, and even a secret garden with a raised marble fountain and pool—check out the blooming schedule on the website), and see a wonderful view of Canandaigua Lake. The Queen Anne–style mansion was the home of financier Frederick Ferris and his wife, Mary Clark Thompson, and you can wander through much of the abode, including the Great Hall, bedrooms, and Billiard and Trophy Rooms. The park also houses the Finger Lakes Wine Center, where you can enjoy tasting tours (seasonal). All kinds of fun events are hosted here, from teas to happy hours to concert series and more (see events calendar).

10 Yaddo Gardens

312 Union Ave., Saratoga Springs, NY 12866; 518-584-0746
www.yaddo.org

Financier and philanthropist Spencer Trask gave Yaddo Gardens to his wife, Katrina, in 1899, and then they designed it together; they created two terraces, divided by a pergola, with the lower section housing a formal Rose Garden (with peak blooms mid-June–July and then in mid- to late August) and the upper one displaying a woodland rock garden (peak is mid-June–mid-September). Each space has a fountain. Admission and parking are free. Garden tours are offered on Saturdays and Sundays and some Tuesdays (in season). Ghost tours are on Friday and Sunday evenings, mid-September–late October. (Credit cards are not accepted.) There's also a self-guided tour (download from website). The Trasks founded Yaddo to support the artists' community; writers James Baldwin and Langston Hughes, along with many others, have visited it.

Garden at the Mohonk Mountain House Resort

Walkway over the Hudson

NEW YORK CONTAINS more than 700 trails, including some well-known ones such as the Appalachian Trail and other paths with spectacular views of the Hudson Valley, the Catskills, and the Adirondacks. There's something for everyone—whether you want to climb all 46 of the Adirondack High Peaks or bike across the Walkway Over the Hudson. Mohonk Preserve alone has 6,500 acres to explore. So go outside and enjoy everything the state has to offer.

HIKING AND BIKING TRAILS

41

1 Black Creek Preserve

Winding Brook Road, Esopus, NY 12429; 845-473-4440
www.scenichudson.org/parks/blackcreek

What a walk: take the Yellow Trail to a 120-foot suspension bridge across Black Creek, through a forest to the Red Trail, and then past old stone walls—remnants from a farm—before coming to the Blue Trail, which leads to the Hudson River shoreline. Despite some uphill climbs, most of the route is family friendly. Depending on the time of year, you might see vernal pools, which form temporarily due to winter runoff, supplying food and helping animals (like wood frogs) to breed. Lots of endangered species are found here, including blue-back herrings and alewives, which come from the ocean to lay their eggs in the creek. Kiosks scattered around the 130-acre preserve offer information on the plants, animals, and creek.

2 Esopus Bend Nature Preserve

4 Shady Lane, Saugerties, NY12477
www.esopuscreekconservancy.org/around_the_bend

This 164-acre preserve along Esopus Creek was once part of the Schroeder farm, even though more than 40 years have passed since crops were grown here. You can see lots of wildlife here—from turkeys in the spring to snapping turtles, beavers, eagles, coyotes, and more. The preserve offers a diverse landscape, with its lowland meadows, wetlands, and sloping and floodplain forests. Besides the four moderately difficult hiking trails and a series of meadow paths that lead to a natural sandbar, the preserve organizes guided nature walks, birding field trips, water tours, and animal tracking (see event calendar and preregister). Leashed dogs are allowed on the Schroeder (part of an old carriage road) and South Trails only. Limited parking is available.

3 | Falling Waters Preserve

996 Dominican Lane, Glasco, NY 12432; 845-473-4440
www.scenichudson.org/parks/fallingwaters

This 149-acre preserve offers stunning views of the Catskills, two small waterfalls that cascade over rocks, and the Hudson River. As you hike, you'll pass the remains of the Mulford Ice House, a windowless building that once stored some 10,000 tons of ice collected from the river—eventually shipping it to New York City. You can read all about the history from a kiosk at the entrance. Walk over several miles of trails, from gravel and riverside paths to an old carriage road. The four trails pass through grassy fields and woods and offer comfortable wooden benches where you can rest while you contemplate nature. The 0.65-mile Riverside Trail is rocky but offers the best views of the Hudson River.

4 | Franny Reese State Park

129 Macks Lane, Highland, NY 12528; 845-473-4440
www.scenichudson.org/parks/frannyreese

This 253-acre park, named after a local environmentalist and activist, contains 2.5 miles of mostly woodland trails, with the 0.87-mile Yellow Trail passing the ruins of the former Cedar Glen estate before moving downhill and under the Mid-Hudson Bridge, where it connects to steep steps that end at Johnson-Iorio Memorial Park. Both the White Trail (1.76 miles) and Blue Trail (0.25 miles) offer some spectacular views of the bridge, the Walkway Over the Hudson (see page 45), and Pough-keepsie. Parking is limited, but the trails are often quiet, especially in the winter and early spring—and you can feel like you're alone in the woods sometimes. The 4.5-mile Walkway Loop Trail is also accessible from the park.

5 | McCauley Mountain

300 McCauley Mountain Road, Old Forge, NY 13420; 315-369-3225
www.mccauleyny.com

Primarily a winter destination for skiers, snowboarders, and those who snowshoe, McCauley Mountain also offers scenic chairlift rides from spring to fall—perfect for catching a view of the Fulton Chain of Lakes and the Adirondack Mountains. An observation deck at the top has seats and tables, so bring a picnic. You'll find a short hiking trail up there too. There are also several trails for those who want to walk up or down McCauley Mountain, which has an altitude of 2,200 feet and 21 ski trails. For mountain bikers, there are 20 miles of trails, some of them new, including rocky singletrack, doubletrack, and flow trails. Kids have their choice of two playground areas.

6 Minnewaska State Park Preserve

5281 US 44/NY 55, Kerhonkson, NY 12446; 845-255-0752
www.parks.ny.gov/parks/127

On the Shawangunk Mountain ridge, some 2,000 feet high, you'll find a variety of terrains, from rocky, rugged areas to waterfalls to sky lakes (pristine bodies of water created from rain), hardwood forests, sheer cliffs, and ledges—along with 35 miles of carriage roads and 50 miles of paths. You'll get a trail map when you enter the 22,275-acre park. Besides hiking, biking, horseback riding, and climbing, there's plenty for water lovers, including boating (nonmotorized only), swimming, and scuba diving. Sam's Point Preserve, the highest section on the mountain, offers panoramic views, a dwarf pine forest, and ice cave exploration. Parking is limited and closes at capacity. (Day fee required.)

7 Mohonk Preserve

3197 US 44/NY 55, Gardiner, NY 12525; 845-255-0919
www.mohonkpreserve.org

Whether you like to bike, hike, cross-country ski, snowshoe, run, rock climb, or ride horses, this preserve with 8,000 acres, 70 miles of carriage roads, and 40 miles of trails provides stunning views of nature, including the Catskill and Shawangunk Mountains. The Visitor's Center (get free maps and tips on how to spend your day, and watch a short film on the area) and its grounds are free to visit (there are several short hiking trails), but everything else requires a day-use fee or membership. Activities such as volunteer-led hikes, guided bike rides, morning bird walks, and yoga are also offered (check the events calendar). Parking fills up quickly (165,000 people visit annually), so get here early, or you might be turned away.

8 Slide Mountain Wilderness

Ulster County, located in the towns of Shandaken, Denning, and Olive, NY;
845-256-3000
www.dec.ny.gov/lands/9150.html

The most-used section of the Catskill Forest Preserve, Slide Mountain contains more than 47,500 acres with over 35 miles of rugged trails in the moderate and challenging categories. More-experienced hikers can ascend the mountain on the Burroughs Range Trail, climbing almost to the Catskill's highest peak at 4,180 feet. The Woodland Valley–Denning Trail follows a carriage road, making for an easier moderate hike. Other trails go through remote forests, offering mountain views and opportunities for backcountry camping. Some of the animals you might see include deer, turkeys, coyotes, and bears. Fishing and hunting (in designated areas) are permitted.

9 Walkway Over the Hudson

Entrances:
87 Haviland Road, Highland, NY 12528; 845-454-9649
61 Parker Ave., Poughkeepsie, NY 12601; 845-834-2867
www.walkway.org

Touted as the longest elevated pedestrian walkway in the world on its website, the former 19th-century railroad bridge allows you to walk over the Hudson River from Poughkeepsie to Highland. The 1.28-mile concrete walkway is 212 feet above the river. You can extend your trip by venturing onto the rail-trail network on either side (some 7 miles of paved Hudson Valley Rail Trail on the west and the 13-mile Dutchess County Rail Trail on the east). Several free (get there early) and fee-based parking areas are located near the walkway. The path—friendly to walkers, bicyclers, skateboarders, and leashed pets—is also accessible by an elevator entrance on Water Street in Poughkeepsie. Restrooms and picnic tables are available at both walkway entrances.

10 Walnut Mountain Park

73 Walnut Mountain Road, Liberty, NY 12754; 845-292-7690
www.townofliberty.org

This 265-acre park in the Catskills offers many hiking and biking trails, formerly old carriage roads, that wind their way through the woods and fields. The land was previously the property of the Walnut Mountain Hotel, and you can still see parts of the foundation and fireplace along the walking trail. The 13 miles of well-marked trails are often steep (Walnut Mountain is the second highest in Sullivan County) but accessible to most abilities—with levels from easy to challenging. At the mountain's base, there's a picnic area with grills, sports fields, a playground, and a pavilion. In the winter, you can snowshoe and cross-country ski.

Boldt Castle

LEARNING ABOUT HISTORY helps us understand ourselves: it explains how society developed, teaches empathy for other generations, and shows the flaws and strengths in humans. New York's past takes you to the battles of the Revolutionary War and the beginnings of a new nation. It inspires you to value creativity, like that of the artists of the Hudson River school, as well as love and loss, as expressed through the story of George and Louise Boldt.

HISTORIC SPOTS

Old Fort Niagara

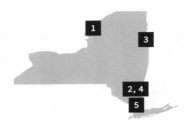

1 Boldt Castle

Collins Landing, Alexandria Bay, NY 13607; 315-482-9724
www.boldtcastle.com

You'll need to take a boat to visit Heart Island, where Boldt Castle is located; many tour operators travel there, and docking is available for private boats. Besides the main building—where you'll find a gift shop and a movie theater on the second floor (see the documentary, which tells the sad love story of hotel magnate George Boldt and his wife, Louise; the air-conditioning is also a respite from summer heat)—there are several gardens and buildings, a fountain, and more. The restored ground floor features beautiful rooms and a grand hallway and staircase, but don't overlook the mazelike basement and its empty swimming pool, along with walls of graffiti left by vandals when the site sat abandoned. There's a café near the docks and picnic areas throughout the grounds. Open May–October.

2 Eleanor Roosevelt National Historic Site

54 Val-Kill Park Road, Hyde Park, NY 12538; 845-229-9422
www.nps.gov/elro

Eleanor Roosevelt is the only first lady with a National Historic Site. Your visit starts with a short film; then a guide will take you on a 45-minute tour of Val-Kill, located about 2 miles from the Franklin D. Roosevelt home. Mrs. Eleanor Roosevelt used this space as a retreat and to develop one of her service projects: helping train rural workers in furniture-making to supplement their incomes. Val-Kill consists of two main buildings, Val-Kill Cottage (which housed Val-Kill Industries, where furniture was made until it closed in 1936), and the Dutch colonial revival–style Stone Cottage. After FDR's death in 1945, Val-Kill became the first lady's primary residence, and in 1977 it became a National Historic Site. On the grounds are gardens and a dollhouse that Eleanor Roosevelt moved from the main house for her grandchildren. Open May–December.

Historic Spots

3 Fort Ticonderoga

102 Fort Ti Road, Ticonderoga, NY 12883; 518-585-2821
www.fortticonderoga.org

Consider purchasing a two-day ticket . . . you just might need the time. This 2,000-acre property, where French and Indian and Revolutionary War battles were fought, offers several tours—including ones that focus on the fort's landscape, the museum, or things families might enjoy. Besides the King's Garden—a walled colonial revival–style collection of flowers, plants, and paths—and the museum exhibitions, you can also tackle the Carillon Battlefield hiking trail; visit historic trade shops where you can watch shoemakers, tailors, and more; wander around a 6-acre corn maze (seasonal); or climb or drive to Mount Defiance, which has views of Lake Champlain, Vermont's Green Mountains, and the Adirondacks. Plus, there are weapons demonstrations, events, reenactments, scenic boat rides (extra cost), a café and shop, and plenty of picnic tables scattered throughout the grounds.

4 Home of Franklin D. Roosevelt National Historic Site

(*Note:* See website for schedule during renovation.)

114 Estates Lane, Hyde Park, NY 12538; 845-229-5320
www.nps.gov/hofr

The birthplace and longtime home of the 32nd president of the United States offers a short film and 1-hour guided tours, where you'll see some of Franklin D. Roosevelt's collections, such as his naval paintings, stuffed birds, and ship models. At the home, officially known as Springwood, you'll look at his childhood bedroom, a music room where autographed photos of famous guests sit on the piano, and more. The 300-acre site also has a rose garden and trails. Also located on the grounds is the Presidential Library and Museum; the first presidential library in the United States, it houses his papers, books, and memorabilia. The site participates in the National Park Service's Junior Ranger program, which allows children to earn a free badge for completing set activities. Roosevelt and his wife, Eleanor, are buried at Springwood.

5 Kykuit

381 N. Broadway, Sleepy Hollow, NY 10591; 914-366-6900
www.hudsonvalley.org/historic-sites/kykuit

At Kykuit—the residence of four generations of Rockefellers, starting with Standard Oil founder John D. Rockefeller—you can really visit two historic homes because all guided tours start at Philipsburg Manor's

Historic Spots

visitor center and sightseers go back and forth to Kykuit on a shuttle bus. There are several tours, from 1.5 to 3 hours long, with all options including the house's main floor and Inner Garden. Art lovers will enjoy the vast collection that includes pieces from Pablo Picasso, Andy Warhol, and Henry Moore. Philipsburg Manor is a living-history museum that takes you back to 1750 when the site was a milling and trading center, and home to 23 slaves. Tour the 300-year-old house, participate in hands-on activities, and speak with guides in period costumes. Open May-November.

6 Minisink Battleground Historic Park

58 County Road 168, Barryville, NY 12719; 845-807-0287
www.minisink.org, www.sullivanny.us/departments/parksrecreation

This 57-acre park honors the men who fought and died at the Battle of Minisink on July 20, 1779—the only Revolutionary War skirmish in the Upper Delaware River Valley. Listed on the National Register of Historic Places, the park has a restroom; places for picnics; a pavilion (a rental fee applies); and three walking trails, including the Battleground Trail, which winds through the historic combat zone. All trails are well maintained, shady, and well signed. Stop first at the Interpretive Center, which offers displays about the battle and information about local plants and animals. You can also pick up trail maps here—all hikes are family friendly. Throughout the park, you'll find interesting stones, such as Indian Rock, where allegedly some of the dead were buried, and the Minisink Battle Monument, which commemorates the fight.

7 National Purple Heart Hall of Honor

374 Temple Hill Road, New Windsor NY 12553; 877-284-6667
www.thepurpleheart.com

This museum honors those who have been awarded the Purple Heart through collecting and sharing their personal stories. Exhibits include an interactive timeline display on conflicts from the Civil War to the present day, artifacts, and oral and videotaped narratives from those who received the medal about their experiences. There is also a database where visitors can search for Purple Heart recipients they know. Check the website for details about the 2020 expansion of the facility.

8 Olana State Historic Site

5720 NY 9G, Hudson, NY 12534; 518-828-1872
www.olana.org

Towering over the town from the hilltop, Olana looks very much like "the center of the world," as Hudson River school artist Frederic Edwin Church described his home and studio. His Persian-style house, with its 250 acres of grounds, offers a network of carriage roads and panoramic views of the Hudson River Valley and the Catskill Mountains. Take a tour of the house or of the grounds; there are several choices available—including a 5-mile driving tour—so check the daily schedule (reservations recommended). If you like to stroll at your own pace, the website offers various audio tours for download. The visitor center has free Wi-Fi and a short, informative film. Olana also hosts art exhibitions in the Evelyn and Maurice Sharp Gallery and events such as speakers, morning yoga, and a summer market.

9 Old Fort Niagara

102 Morrow Plaza, Youngstown, NY 14174; 716-745-7611
www.oldfortniagara.org

Sitting on the Niagara River, the fort provided a strategic post for more than 300 years, with the French creating its first iteration, Fort Conti, in 1679. The British took Fort Niagara, now an impressive fortification, in 1759 during the French and Indian War, and it finally came under permanent American ownership in 1815. While there, you'll tour historic buildings, see (and hear!) musket demos, and learn about what life was like for soldiers during the 18th and 19th centuries. Start at the visitor center for exhibits, including the fort's original flag from the War of 1812, and a 16-minute film. Scheduled reenactments of events, such as battles and encampments, immerse you in the history; check the calendar online. Lunch and snacks are available in the log cabin during the summer. The fort is open year-round.

10 Saratoga National Historic Park

648 NY 32, Stillwater, NY 12170; 518-664-9821
www.nps.gov/sara

When British General John Burgoyne surrendered in 1777 to American forces at Saratoga, it was a pivotal victory for the patriots—and the turning point of the American Revolution. Start your trip at the visitor center and collect a map and brochure. There's also a 20-minute film, a 15-minute fiber-optic light map explaining the Battle of Saratoga's importance, a store, some artifacts on display, and a restroom. To see the battlefield, you can access several tours through a mobile web app

(sara.toursphere.com), your cell phone (call 518-665-8185 at each of the 10 road stops), by downloading MP3 audio files for kids and adults (see the multimedia-presentations section at the website), or by hiring a prearranged tour guide. Some places you'll see are the Schuyler House, the 155-foot obelisk commemorating the battle, and the 22-acre Victory Woods.

11 Thomas Cole National Historic Site

218 Spring St., Catskill, NY 12414; 518-943-7465
www.thomascole.org

Catch a view of the Catskills from Thomas Cole's porch, and you can gain insight about the lighting and landscape that inspired the artist who founded the Hudson River school, the first major art movement in the United States, according to the site's website. The complex offers guided tours (before 2 p.m.) and explore-on-your-own visits (after 2 p.m.) of his three-story 1815 federal-style home and studio, exhibitions of paintings (see schedule for current shows), a garden, and a multimedia presentation on Cole's art. The visitor center—housed in the 1839 barn that also holds Cole's Old Studio, where he worked from 1839 to 1846 and where you can see his easels and tools—includes a shop, restroom, and welcome area where you can purchase tickets (seasonal).

12 U.S. Military Academy at West Point

606 Thayer Road, West Point, NY 10996; 845-938-4011
www.westpoint.edu

All tours start at the visitor center, where you'll board a bus for a 1-hour-and-15-minute or 2-hour tour and learn the history of West Point, from its days as a Revolutionary War post to the military academy it subsequently became. The longer tour also visits the cemetery and the Old Cadet Chapel—this tour requires more walking, parts of it on unpaved and uneven ground. A free museum containing military artifacts, such as a sword once carried by Napoleon, the last message from Lt. Col. George A. Custer at the Battle of Little Big Horn, historic uniforms including jungle fatigues worn in Vietnam, and displays on topics such as the Gulf War and the Manhattan Project. Security is tight, so bring a government-issued photo ID if you're over age 17.

13 Vanderbilt Mansion National Historic Site

119 Vanderbilt Park Road, Hyde Park, NY 12538; 845-229-7770
www.nps.gov/vama

Take a 45- to 60-minute guided tour—beware, summer weekends, holidays, and October can sell out—of a 54-room Beaux-Arts–style mansion that still has many of its original furnishings and is a wonderful example of a Gilded Age country house. You'll learn about its architecture as well as the history of its owners—Frederick, grandson of shipping and railroad tycoon Cornelius Vanderbilt, and his wife, Louise. Roam the 211-acre grounds, which include an Italian Garden (where you can geocache; see geocaching.com), expansive lawns, and sweeping views of the Hudson River and Catskill Mountains. If you have time, walk to Bard's Rock, which juts out over the Hudson. The Vanderbilt family donated the property, also known as Hyde Park, to the National Park Service in 1940 after President Franklin D. Roosevelt suggested the idea to Frederick's heir.

The Vanderbilt Mansion National Historic Site in Hyde Park, New York

`14` Washington Irving's Sunnyside

3 West Sunnyside Lane, Irvington, NY 10533; 914-366-6900 weekdays,
914-591-8763 weekends
www.hudsonvalley.org/historic-sites/washington-irvings-sunnyside

Celebrate the author, also a historian, who created the legends of
sleepy Rip Van Winkle and the Headless Horseman. His restored
home and grounds, once a Dutch farm, display original furnishings
such as the oak desk he wrote on and part of his book collection. Guides in period dress tell stories of Irving's life, home—he
spent much of his time there—and literature legacy. You can
see the Hudson River from his porch, or the "piazza," as Irving
dubbed it. A gift shop sells souvenirs and copies of his work. Open
May–November,Sunnyside celebrates Halloween with activities, a
scavenger hunt, spooky tales, and historic games (for more information, see www.hudsonvalley.org/events/home-of-the-legend).

`15` Washington's Headquarters State Historic Site

84 Liberty St., Newburgh, NY 12551; 845-562-1195
www.parks.ny.gov/historic-sites

While stationed at these headquarters in 1782–83, General George
Washington, commander of the Continental Army, helped shape the
American republic, ended the fighting of the Revolutionary War, and
rejected the idea of an American monarchy. Visit the fieldstone farm-
house, also called Hasbrouck House, which offers guided tours. You'll
also want to spend some time in the on-site museum, featuring two
floors of exhibits containing more than 1,300 objects. You'll leave the
place knowing more about the man who became our first president.
After touring, wander the grounds, and then climb the 130-year-old,
53-foot-tall Tower of Victory—it's worth tackling the narrow spiral
staircase that leads to the belvedere for the views of the Hudson
River and Mount Beacon. Open April–October.

Historic Spots

A statue of George Washington in front of Washington Hall at the
U.S. Military Academy, West Point

At the Great Jack O'Lantern Blaze

THERE'S NOTHING LIKE a holiday—a break from the routine of life and an opportunity to try new activities and adventures. Halloween spooks and chills are especially fun. You can scare yourself with tales of terror and spirits—or go ghost hunting in a historic poorhouse. Celebrate the yuletide season with festivals that fete gingerbread houses, the Christmas classic *It's a Wonderful Life,* Sinterklaas, and much more.

HOLIDAY FUN

1 Erie Canal Museum Gingerbread Gallery

318 Erie Blvd. E., Syracuse, NY 13202; 315-471-0593
www.eriecanalmuseum.org/gingerbread

The Erie Canal Museum is open year-round and educates the public about the Erie Canal's importance to industry and the area. When it held its first gingerbread showcase in 1986, no one could have predicted what a hit it would become. Now a six-week event, it features gingerbread houses, shops, trains, and more made by local bakers, aka "Gingerbread Architects." (Want to join in? Fill out the interest form on the website.) The museum also holds culinary events like a Gingerbread Build and Sip, providing supplies such as graham crackers and edible decorations and offering a cash bar and holiday music, as well as gingerbread-house workshops for kids. The exhibition has a grand opening in late November with cookies, cocoa, and music, and the show runs through early January.

2 Farmers Museum Candlelight Evening

5775 NY 80, Cooperstown, NY 13326; 607-547-1450
www.farmersmuseum.org

Journey back to a simpler time at the annual Candlelight Evening, where candle luminaries and greenery decorate this living-history museum. You'll hear the jingle of bells as horses pull wagons with attendees through the grounds. Enjoy a bonfire on the Tavern Green, and sample a cup of wassail, warm cider with a scent that permeates the village as it's heated in kettles on open fires. St. Nick reads "'Twas the Night Before Christmas," and dramatic renditions of *A Christmas Carol* are performed. Best of all is the festive music: local bands play holiday classics, and there's sing-along caroling. The Farmers Museum showcases the area's agricultural heritage through interactive exhibits where you can wander through a working farmstead and a 19th-century village and participate in activities like setting type on an old printing press.

3 Ghost Stories of the Beekman Inn

The Beekman Arms Inn, 6387 Mill St., Rhinebeck, NY 12572; 845-876-7077
www.beekmandelamaterinn.com

Visit the Beekman, an inn since 1766, and tour parts of it that guests never see. You'll end up in the basement to commune with the 250-year-old ghosts who frequent what the website asserts is America's oldest continuously operated hotel. (Well, you'll hear the spirits' tales at least.) "Ghost Stories in the Basement" is intended for mature audiences only, runs Fridays throughout the year (see events calendar for specifics); tours can also be scheduled anytime for groups of 10 or more. The inn has quite the history—during the American Revolution, the Fourth Regiment of the Continental Army did drills on the front lawn, and dignitaries such as George Washington and Alexander Hamilton slept here. Later, President Franklin Delano Roosevelt would also become a frequent guest. Even Oprah Winfrey has visited the inn.

4 The Great Jack O'Lantern Blaze at Van Cortlandt Manor

525 S. Riverside Dr., Crotonon-Hudson, NY 10520; 914-631-8200
www.hudsonvalley.org/events/blaze

This yearly event showcases more than 7,000 hand-carved pumpkins that illuminate the grounds of Van Cortlandt Manor like a Halloween art installation. You'll see various arrangements and themes—some are conceptual, while others celebrate famous superheroes or actors. The show uses synchronized lighting and an original soundtrack to heighten the experience. It takes about an hour to walk through the exhibit, depending on the crowd and your pace. The Blaze, as it's called for short, started in 2005. Real and fake pumpkins are used, with the carving of the mock ones starting in June; the real pumpkins are designed about a week prior to opening and then throughout the seven-week run. A gift shop sells everything pumpkin, along with fall treats, clothing, and LED items so that you, too, can light up the dark.

Holiday Fun

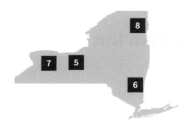

5 *It's a Wonderful Life* Festival

32 Fall St., Seneca Falls, NY 13148; 315-568-5838
www.therealbedfordfalls.com, www.wonderfullifemuseum.com

Dubbed "the Real Bedford Falls," Seneca Falls celebrates the beloved movie with a festival during the second weekend in December. The *It's a Wonderful Life* Museum & Archives offers a 1.3-mile walking tour brochure that takes you through Seneca Falls, which the museum and locals believe was the inspiration for the movie because of its small-town atmosphere and the fact that Frank Capra allegedly visited Seneca Falls while writing the script. Festival events include screenings, shows, exhibits (including a gingerbread-house competition), presentations based on the film, a 5K run, and shopping in the Bailey Park Vendor Village. The museum, which opened in 2010, is open year-round. Its artifacts include photographs and memorabilia donated by Karolyn Grimes, the actress who played Zuzu, along with other items.

6 Old Dutch Church Cemetery Tours

272 Wall St., Kingston, NY 12401; 845-475-7973
www.theatreontheroad.com

On Saturday nights in October, this historic cemetery tells stories about the revolutionary history of Kingston, its leaders, and the ghosts left behind. The 1-hour tour starts in 1659; by the time it's finished, you'll will be in 1910 and a half-dozen one-time Kingston residents will have spoken to you, recounting their tales—including a young man who died in the Esopus-Indian Wars, a Civil War hero, and a 19th-century Old Dutch Church clergyman and historian. Theatre on the Road presents Living History Cemetery Tours in cooperation with the Old Dutch Church; private tours are available for 20 or more people. The Old Dutch Church is a National Historic Landmark designed in the Renaissance revival style and built in 1852 using local bluestone.

7 Rolling Hills Asylum

11001 Bethany Center Road, East Bethany, NY 14054; 585-502-4066
www.rollinghillsasylum.com

The Genesee County Poor House, a government facility, was established in 1827 to care for widows, orphans, the mentally ill, the destitute, and others. When someone died who had no family, the person was buried on the premises—sadly, there are more than 1,700 documented deaths. Ghost hunting isn't just for Halloween, and you can participate in public or private ghost hunts, guided tours, theme nights (like those geared to classic horror films), and programs featuring paranormal investigators year-round. No worries if you don't have paranormal equipment: an add-on provides a kit that includes a full-spectrum camera, a Mel Meter (which measures electromagnetic fields and temperatures), and training. TV shows such as the Travel Channel's *Ghost Adventures* have featured the site.

8 Santa's Workshop

324 Whiteface Memorial Hwy., Wilmington, NY 12997; 518-946-2211
www.northpoleny.com

Send letters to St. Nick at a real post office, visit his famous reindeer, and say hello to Santa at his house. Since 1949, this child-size version of the alpine village at the North Pole has offered a destination where Christmas comes every day. Located on the scenic Whiteface Mountain Veterans Memorial Highway, Santa's Workshop is charmingly kitschy, with its Christmas Tree Ride, Santa's Sleigh Coasters, and Jack Jingle Theater Museum—all in all, a throwback to a more innocent time. There are all sorts of shows, too, like a nativity pageant and a musical revue. Be sure to visit the frosty North Pole for a photo op. Check the website for special weekends and events, such as Christmas in July. You can also order personalized letters from Santa, mailed from the North Pole.

Holiday Fun

9 Sinterklaas Festival

Produced by Hudson Valley Community Productions
118 La Bergerie Lane, Red Hook, NY 12571
www.sinterklaashudsonvalley.com

Celebrated on different days in Kingston and Rhinebeck, the Sinterklaas Festival lets children become kings and queens, wearing crowns and branches and carrying stars. Based on the real-life St. Nicholas (AD 270–343), a Greek bishop honored by Catholics as the patron saint of children, Sinterklaas is a traditional Dutch folk character who brings gifts to good boys and girls on Christmas; Dutch immigrants brought him along when they settled in the Hudson Valley more than 300 years ago, and he helped inspire the figure now known as Santa Claus in North America. Today's Sinterklaas Festival is nondenominational and inclusive, seeking to unify neighborhoods. You'll find a calendar of events on the website—including tours, crown-and-branch workshops, exhibits, and holiday shopping. The festival has more than 250 entertainers, such as magicians, musicians, and actors. The fun begins with a Send-Off Celebration in Kingston, from which Sinterklaas leaves on a week-long voyage across the Hudson to the village of Rhinebeck, which then hosts a variety of events throughout town. The culminating event is the parade, which features puppets and hundreds (if not thousands) of stars, held aloft by the crowd.

Rolling Hills Asylum

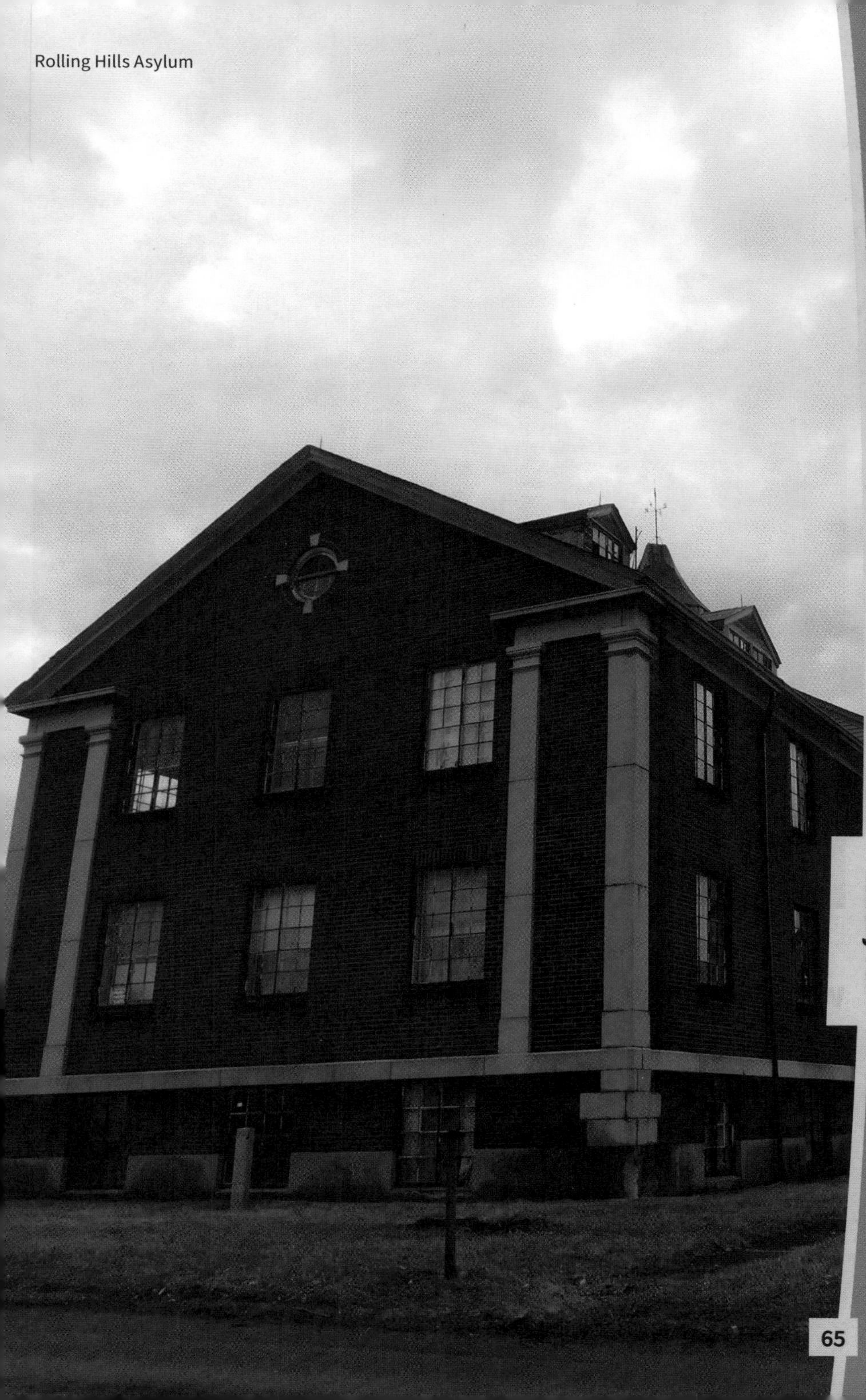

Drime Temple

WHETHER YOU WANT to get away and breathe or you need to revamp your lifestyle to make it healthier, New York State has destinations that showcase historic remedies (like Saratoga Springs' mineral waters and baths) and help you learn to live your best life (YO1 and Kadampa Meditation Center). Some places, such as Lily Dale, offer a place for education and revitalization— and a chance to hear from departed loved ones again.

HOLISTIC EXPERIENCES

1 Kadampa Meditation Center

47 Sweeney Road, Glen Spey, NY 12737; 845-856-9000
www.kadampanewyork.org

You can explore Buddhism and meditation here. First, there's the tranquil World Peace Temple—a perfect place for thinking and recharging. Meditation classes and retreats (including silent ones) are available, and you can also take a tour. On-site accommodations (from private to shared to camping options) and home-cooked vegetarian meals are available. The lush 82-acre grounds offer gardens and nature trails. You'll also find a bookstore and gift shop—full of Buddhist artwork, materials on meditation and Buddhism, and prayer volumes—and the World Peace Café, where you can get local coffee, light meals, and baked goods. You can take classes at the center or one of its satellite facilities; check the website for locations and an events calendar.

2 Lily Dale Assembly

5 Melrose Park, Lily Dale, NY 14752; 716-595-8721
www.lilydaleassembly.org

A 160-acre town in western New York, Lily Dale is where some 22,000 people—seeking wisdom, healing, or communion with the dead—visit during its summer season (end of June through the day before Labor Day). Initially a tent community for spiritualists founded in 1879, the area has evolved into something of a New Age destination that offers educational workshops, stores, a museum, a healing temple, mediumship demonstrations, butterfly releases, and readings from mediums and spiritualists. There are several guest homes, two hotels, and a camping ground and RV park. To visit Lily Dale in the summer, you need a gate pass, something not required off-season, though there are fewer activities and some facilities are closed then.

3 | Saratoga's Mineral Springs and Baths

Various sites around Saratoga Springs, NY; 518-587-3241
www.saratogaspringsvisitorcenter.com

Are you thirsty? Saratoga has more than a dozen public mineral springs for the sampling. The water at most of these springs is naturally carbonated, but it's said that no two springs have water that tastes the same, as the mineral makeup varies. That affects not only the water's flavor but also its alleged health benefits—the water at Old Red Spring, for instance, was once renowned for healing skin conditions. Make sure you bring a cup or bottle with you for tasting. The **Roosevelt Baths & Spa at the Gideon Putnam** (866-890-1171, www.gideon-putnam.com), the last remaining historical baths in the area, offers various therapies, but the Saratoga Springs Heritage Area Visitor Center has a downloadable brochure listing all of the spring sites: go to www.saratogaspringsvisitorcenter.com/maps-brochures and click the link for the mineral waters brochure.

4 | YO1

420 Anawana Lake Road, Monticello, NY 12701; 855-200-6004
www.yo1.com

YO1 wants to help you find a healthier way of living your life. The wellness resort and spa, on 1,300 acres of lakes and pine forests, starts your journey with a wellness counselor who will create a customized program geared toward your goals. Each day consists of scheduled classes and treatments based on holistic Indian therapies such as Ayurveda and naturopathy, as well as yoga and acupuncture. In between those, you can take a dip in the pool, enjoy the sauna, or bike/walk the two trails. Your meals, while not overly filling, are beautiful creations made with organic ingredients; there's also a juice bar. Accommodations are lush, with comfortable rooms and mindful touches like a heated towel rack in the bathroom and robes and slippers.

Holistic
Experiences

Hudson-Athens Lighthouse

NEW YORK STATE, with its rich maritime history, provides a wonderful place to explore lighthouses. Constructed at strategic points, warning vessels of dangerous areas or entry points to rivers and harbors, these romantic beacons feature varied architecture and pristine views. While a few are privately owned, some are open to the public—allowing visitors to climb all the way to the light tower. Others have become museums, offering opportunities to learn about the eras when lighthouses were necessary. Some continue to guide ships even in this modern age.

Albany
Albany Intl. Arpt. (ALB)
SHAKER
OLD NISKAY RD
Maple Wood
Pruyn House
Newtonville
Siena Coll.
Watervliet
Waterlviet Mus.
Hart-Cluett House
Watervliet
Russell Sage Coll.
Prospect Park

LIGHTHOUSES

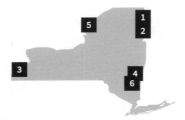

1 Bluff Point Lighthouse

Valcour Island, Plattsburgh, NY 12903; 518-561-0340
www.clintoncountyhistorical.com/bluff-point-lighthouse

This lighthouse, also known as the Valcour Island Light, is in Lake Champlain on Valcour Island. One of the last lighthouses on the lake to be manned, it was active from 1874 to 1930 and guided maritime traffic through the channel between Valcour Island and the New York shore. In 2004, the lighthouse was reactivated. Learn about the only lighthouse on the lake that's listed on the National Register of Historic Places by taking a tour (Sundays in July and August only) to see the building, its Fresnel lens, and the view from the lantern room. You'll hear all about the lighthouse and the keeper's family life, as well as the history and geology of the island; the island also has several hiking trails. It's accessible by boat only.

2 Champlain Memorial Lighthouse

21 Grandview Dr., Crown Point, NY 12928; 518-597-3603
www.historiclakes.org/crown_pt/champlainlight.htm

Named to honor the French explorer, this neoclassical-style lighthouse, with eight Doric columns, was constructed on the base of an earlier limestone tower, the Crown Point Lighthouse, as a memorial to Samuel de Champlain. Completed in 1912, it was deactivated in the mid-1920s, having served as a lighthouse for only a little more than a decade. Now part of the Crown Point State Historic Site, which contains the ruins of Fort St. Frederic, a museum, and walking paths, the lighthouse also features sculptures, including *La France,* a bronze bust by Auguste Rodin. The grounds are open year-round; the museum has a seasonal schedule.

3 Dunkirk Historical Lighthouse and Veterans Park Museum

1 Lighthouse Point Dr. N., Dunkirk, NY 14048; 716-366-5050
www.dunkirklighthouse.com

The 27-mile reach of the light shows the power of its 61-foot Fresnel lens—only 70 of which are still used in the United States. The museum contains military artifacts from WW1 and WW2 and the Korean War, as well as information about the site's history—in fact, the first shot of the War of 1812 rang out near the structure's west bank. Built in 1826, the lighthouse helped ships come into Dunkirk Harbor safely, but by 1875 the tower had fallen into disrepair, and a new stone one with a Victorian residence replaced it. You can explore the lighthouse, climb to the top, and gaze at Lake Erie from the observation deck. The facility also offers seasonal ghost hunts and festivals. Open from May to October.

4 Hudson–Athens Lighthouse

Hudson, NY 12534; 518-828-5294
www.hudsonathenslighthouse.org

This two-story second empire–style brick lighthouse sits in the Hudson River between the towns of Hudson and Athens. Opened in 1874 to protect boats from the treacherous Middle Ground Flats sandbar, the lighthouse was automated in the 1950s. You can view the lighthouse by taking a boat tour—from either the Henry Hudson Riverfront Park or the Athens Waterfront Park—to explore its three levels and eight rooms. After climbing metal stairs, you'll enter the lighthouse and learn about its history through guides and videos. Tours take place the second Saturday of the month from July to October.

5 Rock Island Lighthouse

Fisher's Landing, NY 13641; 315-775-6886
www.parks.ny.gov/parks, www.rockislandlighthouse.org

One of six lighthouses along the St. Lawrence River, this one helped guide ships to and from Lake Ontario from 1847 to 1955. The island and its buildings opened as a public park in 2013, and the 19th-century keeper's house was transformed into a maritime museum about the island's history, including the seaway's importance as a transportation route. Climb the circular staircase to the top, and enjoy a view of the river from the lantern room. You can picnic on the grounds; a gift shop and restrooms are also on-site. Located on Rock Island between Alexandria Bay and Clayton, the lighthouse is accessible (in season) by boat only.

6 Rondout Lighthouse

50 Rondout Lndg., Kingston NY 12401; 845-338-0071
www.hrmm.org/rondout-lighthouse.html

One of only seven lighthouses still standing on the Hudson River, the Rondout Lighthouse was built three times: the original wooden structure was built in 1837; then a stone one replaced it in 1867 (look for

remnants of the foundation when you visit) but was eventually abandoned. The current brick version opened in 1915. Only accessible by boat, the facility offers guided tours of the first floor to the observation deck on weekends from June to October through the Hudson River Maritime Museum. *Note:* The lighthouse has many stairs (and is therefore inaccessible to wheelchairs), a ladder, and no restrooms, so plan accordingly.

7 Saugerties Lighthouse Trail

168 Lighthouse Dr., Saugerties, NY 12477; 845-247-0656
www.saugertieslighthouse.com

The family-friendly half-mile trail features a mixture of earth, sand paths, and wooden boardwalks. Portions of the trail flood twice a day, so check the tide table at the entrance or on the website before venturing out. The 10-minute walk ends at the Saugerties Lighthouse, built at the mouth of Esopus Creek in 1869. Twenty-minute guided tours, conducted on Sunday afternoons from Memorial Day through Labor Day, noon–3 p.m., include a visit to the museum (formerly a bedroom) and a glimpse of the view from the tower. The deck next to lighthouse is furnished with picnic tables for the public. The lighthouse also houses a bed-and-breakfast that books up months in advance—all guests must arrive on foot or by private boat for their stay.

8 Stony Point Lighthouse/Battlefield Historic State Site

44 Battlefield Road, Stony Point NY 10980; 845-786-2521
www.parks.ny.gov/historic-sites

Located on the grounds of the Stony Point Battlefield Historic Site, this octagonal stone lighthouse rests on a peninsula in the Haverstraw Bay. For 99 years, from 1826 to 1925, the oldest lighthouse on the Hudson River helped boats navigate the waters. Only once, in 1901, did a boat—the steamer *Poughkeepsie*—run aground, and even then no one was killed. The site includes a museum about the lighthouse and the Battle of Stony Point, one of the final battles in the Revolutionary War for the northeastern colonies. Enjoy interactive

Lighthouses

programs by watching cooking and blacksmith demonstrations, along with military reenactments and cannon and musket firings. You can also see a rare Fresnel lens inside the museum.

9 Tibbetts Point Lighthouse

33435 County Road 6, Cape Vincent, NY 13618; 315-654-2700
www.capevincent.org/lighthouse

Marking the place where Lake Ontario meets the St. Lawrence River, the Tibbetts Point Lighthouse contains an original Fresnel lens—made much thinner than regular ones to increase the lighthouse's visibility—and the only original working one in Lake Ontario. While you can't climb to the top, there's a telescope to check out the view, along with a small museum. The lighthouse's first tower and keeper's quarters were built in 1827 after Captain John Tibbetts donated 3 acres to the government. In 1984, the Victorian-era quarters became a hostel for overnighters. Open from Memorial Day weekend to Columbus Day.

Tibbetts Point Lighthouse

Lighthouses

FASNY Museum of Firefighting

YOU DON'T NEED to visit the big city to see high-caliber museums full of novel experiences and engaging exhibits. Some offer interactive displays, like the Adirondack Experience, which allows you to paddle vintage boats, or the FASNY Museum of Firefighting, where you can see how difficult it was for a bucket brigade to put out a fire. Others celebrate famous individuals like TV legend Lucille Ball or painter Edward Hopper. All educate and entertain—so take a look.

MUSEUMS

1 Adirondack Experience: The Museum on Blue Mountain Lake

9097 NY 30, Blue Mountain Lake, NY 12812; 518-352-7311
www.theadkx.org

The Adirondacks have considerable history—and this museum shows it in an unusual way. The 121-acre indoor/outdoor facility lets you wander around its 23 buildings to experience what living in the Adirondacks meant, from stepping on a giant walk-on map to breaking up a logging jam to doing laundry on a washboard in the Kids Cabin—plus more conventional galleries and exhibits showing the Adirondacks from its beginnings to its importance in various industries. Try hiking the 0.75-mile Minnow Pond Trail to the ADKX Boathouse, where you can rent vintage boats, guideboats, or rowboats. Feed the trout and watch the boat-builder-in-residence do construction demonstrations. The on-site Lake View Café serves lunch and snacks. Open from May to October.

2 Corning Museum of Glass

One Museum Way, Corning, NY 14830; 800-732-6845
www.cmog.org

You'll need at least 3–4 hours to see everything in this museum—which comprises some 50,000 objects—but don't worry: tickets are valid for two consecutive days. You'll find 35 centuries of glass, including Near Eastern, Asian, European, and American pieces from antiquity to contemporary times. In the Innovation Center, you learn how glass impacted the world, and activity stations let you bend light and glass and even look through a periscope at Corning. There are also glassmaking demonstrations, lectures, guided tours, and an extra-cost make-your-own-glass opportunity (price depends on the project). Classes in glassblowing and stained glass making are available as well; the museum also has a café, a noncirculating research library, and a shop that features original work from more than 200 artists.

3 Edward Hopper House Museum & Study Center

82 N. Broadway, Nyack, NY 10960; 845-358-0774
www.edwardhopperhouse.org

Stand on the same polished wooden floorboards that American realist painter Edward Hopper roamed at his birthplace and family home. Then look out his bedroom window at the views of Nyack and the Hudson River that he saw for 28 years of his life. The museum, which became a nonprofit art center in 1971, is full of family photographs, handwritten notes, and Hopper's art and memorabilia. Gallery space for artists hosts rotating exhibitions. Concerts, lectures, and special events occur throughout the year, and family art workshops are conducted on most weekends. The gift shop sells books, postcards, and posters of Hopper's artwork and displays the work of the artist of the month. A backyard sculpture garden hosts live jazz concerts in the summer.

4 FASNY Museum of Firefighting

117 Harry Howard Ave., Hudson, NY 12534; 518-822-1875
www.fasnyfiremuseum.com

This museum, a facility of the Firemen's Association of the State of New York, is home to an amazing collection of vintage fire trucks and gear, including interesting tools you've never heard about—like the bed keys used by colonial firemen to quickly disassemble those valuable sleeping spots to save them. Children will enjoy meeting the museum's dalmatian mascot, Molly Williams, named for the first female volunteer firefighter; trying the beat-the-clock Bucket Brigade activity (will they grab enough water to put the fire out in time?); and completing the Junior Firefighter Challenge course, with activities like sliding down a pole. Super Saturdays (see website for calendar) offer special programs such as story times and meet-and-greets. Parents will have fun, too, looking at exhibits like Currier and Ives lithographs celebrating firefighters and the "Then, Now, and Always" display, showing the development of firefighting from ancient times through the 1900s.

5 George Eastman Museum

900 East Ave., Rochester, NY 14607; 585-327-4800
www.eastman.org

Step into the world of George Eastman, camera and film innovator. His colonial revival mansion—which he lived in until his death in 1932—features more than 200,000 original furnishings and artifacts, including photographs and films (the facility has more than 28,000 titles from Thomas Edison's first Kinetoscope efforts to current times).

Wander around on your own, or take a tour. For kids, there's the Discovery Room, where they can use light-sensitive paper to create images—no camera necessary. You'll also find five restored garden areas designed according to estate photos, along with original architectural drawings and correspondence descriptions. Screenings of classic films are offered at the 500-seat Dryden Theatre, one of the few venues left with a projection booth that can show 35-millimeter nitrate prints. Events and educational opportunities are offered, too, including talks, workshops, and live music.

6 Lucille Ball Desi Arnaz Museum

2 W. Third St., Jamestown, NY 14701; 716-484-0800
www.lucy-desi.com

Honoring the influential work of Lucille Ball and Desi Arnaz, the stars of *I Love Lucy,* this museum, located in Ball's hometown, began in 1996. You can see costumes, photographs, and Emmys from their careers or listen to audio clips from Arnaz's autobiography, *A Book,* and tales of Ball's youth recorded from childhood friends. You'll also learn about the impact and history of Desilu Studios, which produced hits like *The Dick Van Dyke Show.* TV buffs will love the replica of Lucy and Ricky Ricardo's living room and the set for the infamous Vitameatavegamin commercial. The museum is part of the National Comedy Center complex (opened in 2018), which tells the history of comedy through interactive exhibits and presents an annual Lucille Ball Comedy Festival in August (past performers include Joan Rivers and Ellen DeGeneres). The gift shop specializes in all things Lucy.

7 Woodstock Museum Inc.

13 Bach Road, Saugerties, NY 12477; 845-246-0600
www.woodstockmuseum.org

Learn all about the history of the famous three-day Woodstock Festival at this small, off-the-beaten path, somewhat-hard-to-find museum. Owner Nathan Koenig will (most likely) guide you through this collection of photography, posters, and memorabilia, recounting stories about the concert from its roots to subsequent music gatherings to the era's history. You'll also see exhibits on Native Americans and *Hipstory*—a film tribute to the 40th anniversary of the 1969 festival. Although it's not the site of the actual concert (go to Bethel Woods for that; see page 127), both hardcore fans and those just learning about the event can enjoy this experience. Open weekends noon–4 p.m.; weekdays by appointment only.

George Eastman House Garden

Iroquois museum with garden

BEFORE EUROPEANS SETTLED New York, more than a dozen Native American tribes called the land home, including the Mohawk, Oneida, Onondaga, Cayuga, Seneca (Seneca Nation and Tonawanda Band of Senecas), Tuscarora, Shinnecock, Abenaki, Munsee, Mohegan, Montauk, Mohican, and Wappinger; today only the first eight (including the two Seneca tribes) are federally recognized. Upstate New York provides many opportunities to experience the rich history and cultural traditions of the famed Six Nations—the Cayuga, Mohawk, Oneida, Onondaga, Seneca, and Tuscarora.

NATIVE AMERICAN CULTURE

1 **Fenimore Art Museum,** *Cooperstown* *84*
You can see lots of American art here, including an American Indian wing with almost 850 items and events showcasing Iroquois culture.

2 **Iroquois Indian Museum,** *Howes Cave* *84*
Explore the history and culture of the Six Nations with child-friendly, interactive exhibits and demonstrations, plus a 45-acre park with trails.

3 **Kanatsiohareke Mohawk Strawberry Festival,** *Fonda* *85*
During the last weekend of June, the Kanatsiohareke Mohawk community hosts an annual two-day festival filled with native traditions.

4 **National Kateri Tekakawitha Shrine and Historic Site,** *Fonda* *85*
This shrine to the first Native American Catholic saint consists of exhibits, a chapel, hiking trails—and a spring with possible healing powers.

5 **Seneca-Iroquois National Museum,** *Salamanca* *85*
This museum houses thousands of Six Nations artifacts, with an emphasis on the history and culture of the Seneca Nation.

6 **Six Nations Indian Museum,** *Onchiota* *86*
Learn about the Six Nations with exhibits of beaded belts, baskets, and canoes, as well as contemporary art and campfire displays, plus a gift shop.

1 Fenimore Art Museum

5798 NY 80, Cooperstown, NY 13326; 607-547-1400
www.fenimoreartmuseum.org

While the museum specializes primarily in American folk and fine art, along with photography documenting Cooperstown from the firm Smith and Telfer and writer James Fenimore Cooper's possessions, it also contains an American Indian wing that opened in 1995 after Eugene and Clare Thaw gave the organization their art collection. The display now contains almost 850 objects and features a broad range of Indian cultures, including those from the Northwest coast, the Southwest, and California. The museum offers events from lunchtime tours to films to performances to lectures. You'll also find programs on Native Americans (check calendar for availability). The museum's research library—focusing on New York State, nearby counties, and Native Americans—houses rare books, manuscripts, and other materials.

2 Iroquois Indian Museum

324 Caverns Road, Howes Cave, NY 12092; 518-296-8949
www.iroquoismuseum.org

This museum, designed in the shape of a longhouse, engages visitors with exhibits and interactive experiences. A children's museum—full of puzzles, giant weave-your-own baskets, a turtle pond, and arts and crafts—has its own floor. You can talk to Native Americans about their traditions, look at contemporary Iroquois art, watch demonstrations and dance performances, and even participate in workshops like stone carving and quilt blocks (see the website for a calendar of events). Every summer there's an annual Iroquois Indian Festival weekend with activities for the whole family. The museum is part of a 45-acre nature park with marked trails and a log house sometimes used for storytelling.

3 Kanatsiohareke Mohawk Strawberry Festival

4934 NY 5, Fonda, NY 12068; 518-673-4197
www.mohawkcommunity.com

Join the Kanatsiohareke Mohawk community at their yearly Strawberry Festival during the last weekend of June. Celebrate the strawberry—called "the Leader of the Berries" because it ripens first in the wild—with a variety of events including music, dance, storytelling, demonstrations, a silent auction, and an arts-and-crafts fair full of handmade items like blankets, jewelry, and musical instruments. Enjoy the heart-shaped berry that allegedly can rejuvenate people while learning about Mohawk culture and the Six Nations. The festival helps the Kanatsiohareke community raise funds for their cultural programs and to maintain their land.

4 National Kateri Tekakawitha Shrine and Historic Site

3636 NY 5, Fonda, NY 12068; 518-853-3646
www.katerishrine.com

The first Native American Roman Catholic saint, Kateri Tekakwitha (1656–1680), a Mohawk woman who converted to Christianity in the 17th century, lived in Caughnawaga most of her young life and was canonized by Pope Benedict XVI in 2012. The site also has an 18th-century Dutch barn with a chapel and artifacts from the only completely excavated Iroquois Indian village, according to the website. The village was discovered on a nearby hill in the early 1950s by Franciscan Friar Thomas Grassmann—who found the stockade post molds where the settlement had been—and then he unearthed the site with volunteers. You can see the outlines of the 12 longhouses and stockade from 300 years ago. Also close by is the spring where St. Kateri was baptized—some claim its waters possess healing powers.

5 Seneca-Iroquois National Museum

82 W. Hetzel St., Salamanca, NY 14779; 716-945-1760
www.senecamuseum.org

Learn all about the history and culture of the Seneca Nation through exhibits and experiences. You can walk through an authentic log cabin that was reassembled in the museum and hear traditional stories. You'll also see all types of artifacts and artwork from the Six Nations, including paintings, antler carvings, and more than 250 baskets. The museum's beadwork collection is the largest on the east coast,

according to their website, and dates back to the 1700s. Look at their calendar for fun family events, such as October's Scary Stories Friday and the annual Holiday Fine Art's Show and Market. The museum also preserves historical documents such as family photographs, publications, and multimedia projects.

6 Six Nations Indian Museum

1462 County Route 60, Onchiota, NY 12989; 518-891-2299
www.sixnationsindianmuseum.com

Originally two rooms, the museum opened during the summer of 1954 and was expanded to look like a traditional bark house. Inside you'll find more than 3,000 artifacts from the Haudenosaunee Confederacy (aka the Six Nations of the Iroquois Confederacy). The museum—started by Ray, Christine, and John Fadden—is still family run and includes many charts and diagrams by the founder and his son. It also features paintings by David Fadden, Ray's grandson. The gift shop carries work by Native Americans, including Mohawk baskets, beadwork, and silver jewelry.

Drums and pelts at the Iroquois Festival

Ausable Chasm Waterfall

THE WORLD IS FULL of amazing things—but nothing sur-
passes what nature has given us. All of the phenomenal locations
in this section took millions of years to develop, starting with
receding glaciers and the subsequent flow of water across the land.
Eventually nature configured the local terrain in beautiful ways—
carving out gorges and canyons, falls and woodlands, craggy
mountains, and waterways. What wonderful places to explore!

NATURAL WONDERS

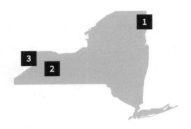

1 Ausable Chasm

2144 NY 9, Ausable Chasm, NY 12911; 518-834-7454
www.ausablechasm.com

Marvel at the power of water when you visit this 500-million-year-old canyon, and see rock formations such as the Elephant's Head and Hyde's Cave. Choose from many adventures. The classic tour contains a 1-mile hike followed by a scenic raft float on the Ausable River, past cliffs and around the Whirlpool Basin, among other sights. For the daring, the Adventure Trail offers a guided *via ferrata* (climbing) course with cable bridges, a cargo net climb, and edge walks. All tours cover the geography and history of the region. There's also rock climbing, rappelling, and a lantern tour, where you'll roast marshmallows deep within the chasm. Mountain bikers will find 15 miles of wooded trails to explore (bike rentals available). A café and gift shop are located at the visitors center; a campground with cabins and RV hookups is also available.

2 Letchworth State Park

1 Letchworth State Park, Castile, NY 14427; 585-493-3600
www.parks.ny.gov/parks/79

The Genesee River courses through a deep gorge and over three signature waterfalls in this nearly 15,000-acre park. Named for William Pryor Letchworth, an iron magnate and philanthropist, the park provides 66 miles of hiking trails—plus opportunities for horseback riding, biking, snowmobiling, and cross-country skiing. Glen Iris, Letchworth's one-time home, is now a restaurant and inn. Don't miss Inspiration Point, the best place to view the river, the 600-foot canyon walls, and two waterfalls—a sight that makes you understand the park's nickname, "the Grand Canyon of the East." A large selection of programming is available, from guided tours, a lecture series, whitewater rafting, and a nature center (with a butterfly garden, and bird and bee observation). The visitor center, located by the Mount Morris Dam, provides restrooms, a shop, food, and picnic areas. On-site cabins, camping, and RV sites are also available.

Niagara Falls

3 Niagara Falls State Park

Visitor Center, 332 Prospect St., Niagara Falls, NY 14303; 716-278-1794
www.niagarafallsstatepark.com

Whether you have a weekend or several days, this 400-acre park provides plenty of activities to fill your time. You can view the falls, getting wet from the Hurricane Deck; hike the paths (download the walking tour app from the App Store or Google Play); learn about the history of the falls with interactive displays at the Discovery Center; explore the ruins of a former power station in the Niagara Gorge; and so much more. Consider purchasing a Discovery Pass if you're interested in experiencing all the attractions, like the *Maid of the Mist* (see page 29) and Cave of the Winds, and you'll get a better rate. The park and falls are free to visit—Frederick Law Olmsted, the creator of Central Park, designed the grounds, which include gardens and more than 15 miles of trails.

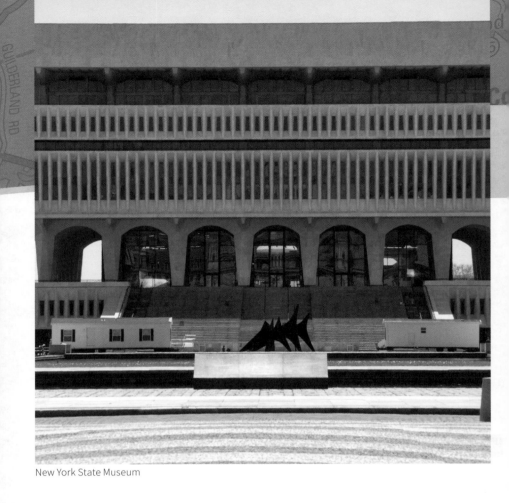

New York State Museum

REMEMBER WHEN? New York is full of locations that celebrate the history of things. You can reminisce about the past, show your children the way the world used to be, or just enjoy revisiting iconic experiences like the drive-in, the arcade—or the delight of Jell-O, fresh maple syrup, or vintage video games.

NOSTALGIA AND OTHER FUN THINGS

1 **Cooperstown Bat Company,** *Hartwick* *94*
Watch a bat-turning demonstration in the factory and hear all about the major
leaguers who have used the company's product line.

2 **Herschell Carrousel Factory Museum,** *North Tonawanda.* *94*
See how carousels are created in a tour that includes some merry-go-rounding
of your own. The outdoor kiddie park offers a bit of nostalgia with antique rides.

3 **House of Frankenstein Wax Museum,** *Lake George*. *94*
Scare yourself silly with this part haunted house, part museum of horror. While
not too scary for the chicken-hearted, it offers enough punch for the more hardcore.

4 **International Maple Museum Centre,** *Croghan*. *95*
Learn the history of maple syrup, from how Native Americans harvested the sweet
liquid to more modern methods. The three-floor museum also has a lumber camp
kitchen replica.

5 **Jell-O Gallery,** *Le Roy* *95*
For dessert lovers everywhere, here's a museum that showcases this much-loved
treat's development—from original advertising art to molds to recipe books.

6 **Kazoo Museum and Factory,** *Eden* *95*
Remember the fun kazoos provided when you were young? Revisit that wonder
while you observe metal ones being created, then buy your own at the gift shop.

7 **Leonelli's Playland Arcade,** *Lake George* *96*
Spend some time reminiscing while you play games like skee-ball and take aim in
the old-school shooting gallery. More contemporary fun is also available for the kids.

8 **New York State Museum,** *Albany*. *96*
The nation's oldest and largest state museum showcases the state—from history
to art, there's even a working carousel from the early 1900s to enjoy.

9 **The Strong National Museum of Play,** *Rochester* *96*
Frolic around at this interactive museum that celebrates play. From *Sesame
Street* to the Berenstain Bears to video games, there's a lot of historic fun here.

10 **Transit Drive-in,** *Lockport*. *97*
One of New York State's largest drive-ins, this family-owned operation features a
snack bar and double features. The family pet can even come along.

1 Cooperstown Bat Company

3152 County Highway 11, Hartwick 13348; 888-547-2415
cooperstownbat.com

Celebrate one of America's favorite pastimes with a factory visit to the company that has been making pro model bats since 1981 for the Major League, American Legion, and other organizations. Bat-turning demonstrations are free to the public Monday through Friday from 9 a.m. to Noon and 1 p.m. to 3 p.m. Learn how wood, like ash or maple, is chosen for each bat, and watch as a piece of wood is turned into the smooth shape of a bat. Workers are happy to answer questions. Groups of 10 or more should call to schedule a tour.

2 Herschell Carrousel Factory Museum

180 Thompson St., North Tonawanda 14120; 716-693-1885
carrouselmuseum.org

Take a ride on the carousel, enjoy vintage kiddie attractions, and learn how carousels are made in this museum that celebrates the merry-go-round with lots of interactive exhibits. Small children will enjoy the outdoor Kiddieland Testing Exhibit as they sample restored antique rides, and the older siblings aren't left out either—with a 1916 Big Carrousel to try and several band organs playing cheery tunes. Check the website for a variety of events, including Lunch with Santa, Children's Book Week, Free Days, and more. Programs for adults (woodcarving classes) and kids (STEM activities) are given as well. Open April through December.

3 House of Frankenstein Wax Museum

213 Canada St., Lake George 12845; 518-668-3377
frakensteinwaxmuseum.com

Watch Frankenstein come to life, a scary séance, witch trials, and a variety of ghastly sights as you wander through the haunted hallways of this house of horrors. The journey is dark, with some strobe lights and quite a few violent images, so parents with young children should keep that in mind. Designed in the spirit of early wax museums, the site offers gross spectacle, a few shocking surprises, and a touch of '80s campiness—all in all, an entertaining walk with the spirits and soulless (seasonal, so check the website for availability).

4 International Maple Museum Centre

9753 State Route 812, Croghan 13327; 315-346-1107
maplemuseumcentre.org

The three floors in the museum cover all aspects of maple syrup production. Visitors will learn about early methodology and see the equipment used for collection. You can also look at replicas of a sugar house, an equipment room, and a logging camp kitchen. There's an American Maple Hall of Fame that recognizes industry standouts too. The audio tour lets you learn at your own pace. Visit the gift shop for maple products and other souvenirs. The Centre hosts periodic pancake and sausage breakfasts that include—what else—real maple syrup. Call for availability.

5 Jell-O Gallery

23 East Main Street, Le Roy 14482; 585-768-7433
jellogallery.org

Learn the history of Jell-O, invented in Le Roy in 1897, with this interactive museum that lets you share your favorite Jell-O story, flavor, and recipe. You'll see original advertising art, molds, memorabilia, toys, and recipe books of this beloved brand of desserts. Can't wait to relive such delicious memories? Check out the website for historic recipes to make Neapolitan Jell-O (1916) or the wartime-inspired Olive Relish (1944). The gift shop offers everything from logo-emblazoned clothes, chef hats, cups, ornaments, and aprons to cookbooks. Open year-round.

6 Kazoo Museum and Factory

8703 South Main St., Eden 14057; 716-992-3960
edenkazoo.com

Just the word kazoo evokes fun. Find out about this instrument's beginnings, fun facts, and how it is made at the only site where metal ones are manufactured in North America. You can see all kinds of kazoos, from wooden samples to those shaped like liquor bottles to gold and silver varieties. If you're inspired, you can even make one of your own for a fee. Call to book your tour in advance (Tuesday through Thursday until 2 p.m. only). The Gift Shop is open Monday through Saturday, 10 a.m.-5 p.m., and features a variety of items, including (of course) kazoos.

7 Leonelli's Playland Arcade

227 Canada St., Lake George 12845; 518-668-5255
playlandarcadelakegeorgeny.com

Oh the fun you'll have playing games in this family-run arcade. After showing the kids the wonder of the vintage shooting gallery, basketball shooting and skee-ball, you can move on to air hockey and all the neon bells and whistles of more contemporary video games. Many of the machines allow you to earn tickets redeemable for a large selection of prizes, including plushies, rubber balls, and lots of other items. You'll need quarters, but there are plenty of change machines to break down those bills.

8 New York State Museum

222 Madison Ave., Albany 12230; 518-474-5877
nysm.nysed.gov

There is so much to see: exhibits on "Adirondack Wilderness" that show how logging and mining impacted the area's ecology; "Bird Hall," dedicated to the state's more than 170 species; and "Black Capital: Harlem in the 1920s" that features the art and culture of the Black Renaissance. Almost every topic is covered, from geology to history to Native Americans to 9/11. There's even a full-size vintage carousel that gives free rides, antique fire engines, and the skeleton of a mastodon. Besides a café and gift shop, the museum offers talks, special days, and other events. Free admission.

9 The Strong National Museum of Play

One Manhattan Square, Rochester 14607; 585-263-2700
Museumofplay.org

You'll find a lot to play with at this museum, which features exhibits such as the National Toy Hall of Fame, the World Video Game Hall of Fame, and the International Center for the History of Electronic Games. There's also the largest indoor butterfly garden in New York to explore, an exhibit on the Berenstain Bears, a game display with more than 15,000 items, puppets that Jim Henson created, all sorts of toys—from dolls to teddy bears to mechanical banks and so much more. Interactivity is encouraged and video game nuts can sample nearly fourdozen historic games.

10 Transit Drive-In

6655 S. Transit Road (Route 78), Lockport 14094; 716-625-8535
transitdrivein.com

Rain or shine, this drive-in, owned and operated by the Cohen family for three generations, brings you back to those *American Graffiti* days. Tune your FM stereo to the frequency listed and watch the flick from the comfort of your car, or bring a portable radio and lawn chairs and enjoy the evening air. Leashed pets welcome. The snack bar features an assortment of treats, including popcorn, burgers, pizza, and candy. You can also play the 19-hole miniature golf. For a good spot on the weekends or holidays, arrive an hour before film time. Despite its size (spots for 1,500 cars), the theater can sell out (seasonal—see website for availability).

Jell-O

Fly Creek Cider Mill & Orchard

TO MARKET, TO MARKET to buy some fresh produce, baked goods, and an assortment of other delightful things. . . . New York has dozens of orchards, family-run farms, and sustainable farmers' markets across the state. Whether you're looking for just-picked fruits, free-range chicken, or a day at the farm, here's a sample of opportunities waiting for you.

ORCHARDS, FARMS, AND FARMERS' MARKETS

1 **Fly Creek Cider Mill & Orchard,** *Fly Creek* *100*
Visit a historic creek-powered mill that offers tours, interactive exhibits, and demos that show how cider is made.

2 **Hudson Farmers Market,** *Columbia County* *100*
For more than 20 years, this farmers' market—Columbia County's largest—has offered fresh food to the public, along with lively music.

3 **Saugerties Farmers Market,** *Saugerties* *101*
More than just shopping, this seasonal market has a kids' art corner, live music, tastings, and other events on Saturdays from May to October.

4 **Stony Creek Farmstead,** *Walton* *101*
Nestled in the beautiful Catskill Mountains, this farm allows stay-over visits where you wander the fields and sleep in platform tents.

1 Fly Creek Cider Mill & Orchard

288 Goose St., Fly Creek, NY 13337; 607-547-9692
www.flycreekcidermill.com

The cider mill on the banks of Fly Creek has been making this sweet drink for more than 160 years, producing 20,000 gallons of it each fall. You can take a self-guided tour, see exhibits and demos, and enjoy tastings. At the Mill Store Marketplace, there are more than 40 foods to sample daily, such as fudge. The Snack Barn Restaurant & Bakery offers a variety of choices, specializing in cider-themed favorites like apple dumplings with cider sauce and cider slush. The facility also holds events such as their annual Antique Engine Show. Kids will love Tractorland, with its trike track and climb-on tractor; feeding ducks at the Millpond; and the vintage collection of John Deere equipment throughout the grounds.

2 Hudson Farmers Market

Municipal lot at the corner of Sixth and Columbia Sts. (outdoor market) or 601 Union St. (indoor market), Hudson, NY 12534; 518-821-2453
www.hudsonfarmersmarketny.com

This market, which opened in 1997 with five vendors, likes to change things up and has guest vendors. New vendors are highlighted on its homepage. At Columbia County's largest farmers' market, you'll find a vast range of items—produce, beer, cheese, baked goods, plants, herbs, honey, mushrooms, fresh flowers, handmade crafts, and so much more. There are community tents (where local individuals, groups, and organizations offer information about projects and initiatives) and entertainment tents (with live music from local artists). Rain or shine, the market runs on Saturdays from April through November and then goes indoors in December and from February through April. Check the website for any schedule changes.

3 Saugerties Farmers Market

115 Main St., Saugerties, NY 12477; 845-681-1160
www.saugertiesfarmersmarket.com

Find fresh and local foods at this seasonal Saturday hotspot (May–October). Located next to the historical DuBois-Kiersted House, the market offers eye-catching views of the Catskill Mountains and all sorts of cheese, pasture-raised meat, free-range poultry, seafood, produce (including dry herbs, orchard fruit, vegetables), baked foods, honey, pickles, and goods ranging from tea to pottery to jewelry to lotions. Local artist Anita Barbour oversees the Kids' Art Corner, where each week she supervises a creative activity. There's also live music, tastings, and special events such as carnivals and Halloween tricks and treats. The on-site café serves lunch and takeout. Enjoy a farm-fresh supper held at a local private home with Annual Harvest Home Dinners that benefit the market; check the website for reservation details.

4 Stony Creek Farmstead

1738 Freer Hollow Road, Walton, NY 13856; 607-865-7965
www.stonycreekfarmstead.com

Three generations of the Marsiglio family have owned and worked this land in the Catskills. Visitors are welcome to eat, shop, tour, or stay here from May through October. Accommodations are off-the-grid platform tents with bunk beds and a separate bedroom with a king-size mattress, plus a kitchen with a wood-burning stove and a small closet with a toilet; to get to the nearby shower house, you'll need to walk over the footbridge. You can cook your own meals or order in from the farm. On Saturday mornings, a guided tour of the facility is available, with evenings reserved for make-your-own pizza and campfires. The store sells free-range meat and vegetables (grown with no chemical fertilizers) as well as weekend boxes.

Orchard's, Farms and Farmers' Markets

Opus 40

A PARK PRIMER: Parks support the community they are in by generating jobs and revenue, improving water and air quality and creating a positive environment where visitors can connect to nature. All these parks offer something special—a bit of unique history or a natural wonder. All are worth a look.

PARKS WITH A TWIST

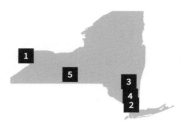

1 Artpark

450 S. Fourth St., Lewiston, NY 14092; 716-754-4375
www.artpark.net

This park, located on the Niagara Gorge, programs more than 150 events over the summer, many of them free of charge. You can watch outdoor concerts and theatrical productions at the 10,000-capacity outdoor amphitheater, with views of the gorge, or the 4,000-seat indoor Mainstage Theater, which has rear gates that open so 2,000 more people can view the performance from the lawn. There's also Music in the Woods, a free Sunday Series in the park's Emerald Grove, which overlooks the Niagara River. Oh, and there's art too. The Percussion Garden lets visitors interact with art creations like the Gong Temple or Chime Tree to make sounds. By the Hopewell burial mound, you'll find a sound installation playing Haudenosaunee (Six Nations) stories and songs. Several art installations are placed throughout the park, and there's also a gallery.

2 Buttermilk Falls County Park

199 S. Greenbush Road, West Nyack, NY 10994; 845-364-2000
www.rocklandgov.com/departments/environmental-resources/county-parks-and-dog-runs/buttermilk-falls-park

The high point, naturally, is Buttermilk Falls, which tumbles down part of the Palisades Ridge. The woods are also beautiful and feature a wide variety of trees like dogwood, hemlock, maple, oak, and sumac. There are many scenic overlooks on the hilltop where you can look at the Ramapo or South Mountains . . . or even New Jersey if it's a clear day. Many visitors have enjoyed the views, including President Teddy Roosevelt, who used to ride horseback in the area. The park has three trails, each less than a mile. Take the Blue Trail from the parking lot to access the falls. (*Tip:* For the best waterfall, schedule your hike after a rainy day.) Dogs are allowed on the trail, which is generally easy to moderate in difficulty but contains some rocky areas—wear good walking shoes.

3 Opus 40

50 Fite Road, Saugerties 12477; 845-246-3400
www.opus40.org

Sculptor Harvey Fite spent 37 years creating this environmental monument where a 9-ton stone monolith rises out of a bluestone quarry under the Overlook Mountain. Using only traditional quarryman's tools such as hammers and chisels, and no mortar or cement, Fite worked rigorously and alone to achieve his vision. Initially, Opus 40's focus was supposed to be Fite's stone carvings, but the setting dwarfed them, and he moved those works throughout the property. Opus 40 is best viewed slowly—take time to look at the sky, water, and stones from different angles. Visit the museum, a collection of Fite's tools, artifacts, and home furnishings, and watch the informative 6-minute video in the art gallery and gift shop. The site offers hiking trails along with many concerts and events; check the website for details.

4 Storm King State Park

Mountain Road, Cornwall-on-Hudson, NY 12520; 845-786-2701
www.parks.ny.gov/parks/152

At Storm King you'll walk along a steep trail, scrambling over rocks as you follow the Orange Trail to the Butter Hill Summit to take in the views—the park offers several awe-inspiring overlooks. Keep that in mind during the hike's beginning as you tough out some of the climb with the most extreme elevation gain. The woodsy trail continues circling 1,300-foot-high Storm King Mountain; you'll proceed to the Blue/Yellow Trails (where you'll find a craggy spot with great views of Newburgh Bay, Bannerman's Castle, the Hudson River, and the Catskills), and then you'll end with the White Trail. There are no restrooms, and limited parking is available, so go early during weekends and summer months. You can hunt in season, but only on the west side of NY 9W.

5 Watkins Glen State Park

1009 N. Franklin St., Watkins Glen, NY 14891; 607-535-4511
www.parks.ny.gov/parks/142

The most famous of the Finger Lakes state parks, 778-acre Watkins Glen offers stunningly beautiful hikes, with miles of trails. On the Gorge Trail, for instance, you'll pass 19 waterfalls and caves as you navigate more than 800 stone steps—there are no handrails, so trekking poles can help make the trip easier (open seasonally; guided tours available). The Rim Trail, open year-round, overlooks the gorge and allows dogs. The terrain varies from ravines to forests. There is camping for tents and trailers, picnic areas, a playground, and an

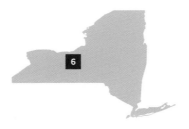

Olympic-size swimming pool. Get ready to hike, cross-country ski, bike, and fish—and bring those binoculars for watching wildlife and birds. There are three entrances (main, south, and north), all with parking and amenities.

6 Women's Rights National Historic Park

136 Fall St., Seneca Falls, NY 13148; 315-568-0024
www.nps.gov/wori

This park is all about the first Women's Rights Convention held July 19 and 20, 1848, in Seneca Falls, and the subsequent movement that followed. Stop at the visitor center for context first, with its exhibits on the history of the women's rights movement and a film. Children can also participate in the Junior Ranger program. The Wesleyan Chapel, the site of the First Women's Rights Convention, and Declaration Park's Waterwall, inscribed with the Declaration of Sentiments—the document enumerating the demands of women in the movement—are next to the center. You can also visit the homes of the movement's leaders, like Elizabeth Cady Stanton, and explore the park's waterways with ranger-guided summer kayak tours. Each year Convention Days are held, where the anniversary of the 1848 Convention is celebrated with speakers and special programs.

Watkins Glen State Park

The Wallkill Rail Trail

THERE ARE ABOUT 110 rail-trails in New York State, according to the Rails-to-Trails Conservancy. For more than 100 years, the railroad was the king of transportation as it helped our communities evolve. Today, these former rail lines provide a touchstone into that time period—with many of these trails offering restored depots, cabooses, and other artifacts as educational spots—and places to walk, bike, and reflect on the beauty of nature.

RAIL-TRAILS

3, 4, 1, 5

1 Hudson Valley Rail Trail

Association: 12 Church St., Highland, NY 12528; 845-691-8588
www.hudsonvalleyrailtrail.net

As you leave the Walkway Over the Hudson (see page 45) on the Highland side, you'll see this 7-plus-mile paved trail, which was once part of the New York, New Haven and Hartford Railroad—and references to its history dot the path. You'll see cabooses from 1915 and 1926, along with train signal towers. The family-friendly walk goes past trees, an abandoned lumber yard, the Hamlet of Highland (where you can pick up lunch), a commemorative garden, a pavilion with restrooms and covered picnic tables, and bridges. The trail offers access to Black Creek and Tony Williams Park, provides a view of Illinois Mountain, and connects to the Wallkill Valley Rail Trail. The HVRT is part of the 750-mile Empire State Trail.

2 O&W Rail Trail

Ulster and Sullivan Counties, NY; 845-292-5111
www.theoandwrailtrail.org

Running along the route once used by the New York, Ontario, and Western Railway (nicknamed the Old and Weary) that first shipped coal and then dairy products, finally closing in 1957, the O&W Rail Trail is best for mountain bikers, hikers, or cross-country skiers. Much of the path is rustic, either grass or dirt, but there is a 2-plus-mile paved section in Hurley appropriate for in-line skaters, as well as wheelchair and scooter users. Other noteworthy sections include Fallsburg's visitor center—the Mountaindale Train Station, located near the trail—with parking, public restrooms, and photos of the original station and a trail section in Parksville with a lovely waterfall on the Little Beaverkill trout stream.

3 Walden-Wallkill Rail Trail

Wooster's Grove, Walden, NY 12586; 845-778-2177
www.villageofwalden.org/departments/parks-and-recreation/walden-parks
/rail-trail

A few miles from the Wallkill Valley Rail, this 3-plus-mile paved rail-trail is ADA compliant and thus appropriate for most nonmotorized activities. Following part of the route of the former Wallkill Valley Railroad—a passenger line that also once transported farmer's goods to New York City—the path goes through the areas of Wallkill and Walden, past farms, forests, and streams. You can start the trail in Walden's Wooster Grove Park, where there is a visitor center, a playground, basketball courts, and plenty of parking. From there you'll continue to the Montgomery–Shawangunk town line, passing the Borden Estate (a mansion built by the granddaughter of Gail Borden, who invented condensed milk) before arriving in Wallkill.

4 Wallkill Valley Rail Trail

Office: 64 Huguenot St., New Paltz, NY 12561; 845-255-2761
www.wallkillvalleylt.org

Journey past small family-owned farms and markets where you can get locally made products, fresh produce, and beverages on the former Wallkill Valley Railroad corridor. While mostly unpaved, except near towns, the gravel, cinder, and packed-dirt 22-plus-mile path can accommodate hybrid or mountain bikers, hikers, cross-country skiers, and horseback riders. You'll go through several towns, from Kingston to Rosendale (where you can see a wonderful view of the Joppenberg Mountain and the Shawangunk Ridge from the 150-foot-tall trestle) to New Paltz, Gardiner, and Wallkill. Along the way are orchards, lakes, streams, and the Wallkill River—so there's plenty of fishing opportunities. The WVRT is part of the 750-mile Empire State Trail.

5 William R. Steinhaus Dutchess Rail Trail

Bowdoin Park Office, 85 Sheafe Road, Wappingers Falls, NY 12590; 845-298-4600
www.dutchessny.gov/departments/parks/dutchess-rail-trail.htm

Perfect for skating, biking, and walking, this 13-plus-mile, wheelchair-accessible asphalt rail-trail takes you from Poughkeepsie to Hopewell Junction. Named after the county executive who supported the development of the former Maybrook Rail corridor, the trail shares a parking lot with Walkway Over the Hudson State Historic Park (see page 45) and goes by Morgan Lake Park, where you can fish. Along the path, you'll pass both new and converted rail bridges and tunnels. A wooded section, the Veterans Memorial Mile in Wappinger, honors the military. In Hopewell Junction, the restored depot, rebuilt after a 1986 fire, is now a museum. The Dutchess Rail Trail is part of the 750-mile Empire State Trail.

Rail-Trails

Cave of the Winds, Niagara Falls

NEW YORK STATE offers a variety of experiences for those who enjoy learning about rocks and minerals (and some great opportunities to collect them). Try rockhounding for Herkimer diamonds, which are not actual diamonds but unique quartz crystals; see why garnet makes such a pretty official state gemstone by touring a mine; or go deep underground, navigate through a cave's tight spaces, and take a subterranean boat ride.

ROCKS AND MINERALS

1 Cave of the Winds

Niagara Falls State Park Visitor Center, 332 Prospect St., Niagara Falls, NY 14303;
716-278-1794
www.niagarafallsstatepark.com/attractions-and-tours/cave-of-the-winds

This experience gets you close to the falls . . . in fact, even with the souvenir sandals and yellow rain ponchos provided, you might get wet. After an elevator takes you down 175 feet into the Niagara Gorge, a guide will lead you through wooden walkways to the Hurricane Deck, where you'll be about 20 feet away from Bridal Veil Falls. You can also visit the World Changed Here Pavilion, an indoor multimedia experience about the falls that shows you how Nikola Tesla harnessed its power, what the falls looked like before becoming an attraction, and more. The Gorge Walk is seasonal, so check the website for dates.

2 Crystal Grove Diamond Mine and Campground

161 County Road 114, St. Johnsville, NY 13452; 518-568-2914
www.crystalgrove.com

Grab a pick and you can hammer into dolomite limestone to look for Herkimer diamonds, quartz crystals specific to certain New York regions. While campers can walk back and forth from their campsites all day and mine until sunset, day miners typically spend 3–6 hours searching for these nearly 500-million-year-old stones shaped like diamonds. The facility excavates the three collecting sites, making digging and scavenging for loose crystals in the dirt a little easier. Note that the mine is not handicap accessible. Be sure to bring boots, goggles, and digging tools (rentals are also available).

3 Garnet Mine Tours

1126 Barton Mines Road, North Creek, NY 12856; 518-251-2706
www.garnetminetours.com

Barton Mines, established in 1878, contains some of the world's largest garnet deposits—the hard, 12-sided stones are unearthed and used as industrial abrasives. Governor Nelson Rockefeller made garnet the New York State gemstone in 1969. For the tour, you'll meet a guide at the Gem & Mineral shop and follow him or her to the mine. Once there, the guide talks about the history and geology of the area and shows you how to find gemstones. After your hunt, it's back to the store to weigh your haul (anything you keep is charged by the pound) and help identify the rocks found. The site has opportunities for shopping and sluicing (where you pan for stones) and an area for picnicking.

4 Herkimer Diamond Mines

4601 NY 28, Herkimer, NY 13350; 315-717-0175
www.herkimerdiamond.com

Become a prospector with all the conveniences of nearby camping, shopping, and dining. Mine for Herkimer diamonds by digging through rocks using hammers and chisels, keeping whatever bounty you find. The facility also contains a Miner's Village (opened in 2018 after a fire destroyed the site's main building), which has a canteen and restaurants. KOA offers tent and cabin sites as well as nifty luxury lodges, including some that contain solar panels, an observatory, or a Japanese garden. There's also sluice mining, where you can pan for fossils, gemstones, or Herkimer diamonds. Visit the Activity Center to create custom jewelry with your newfound treasures.

5 Howe Caverns

255 Discovery Dr., Howes Cave, NY 12092; 518-296-8900
www.howecaverns.com

This destination makes cave sightseeing easy—an elevator takes you down 156 feet to a lit brick path where a guide supervises your walking tour and boat-ride exploration of the 6-million-year-old caves. Want more of an authentic experience? There are also Lantern and Family Flashlight Tours. For the adventurous, a Signature Rock Discovery Tour showcases terrain that Lester Howe, the Schoharie County farmer who discovered the cave, traveled in 1843. To crawl through the tight spaces, you'll need to wear boots, a helmet, and other gear. There's also an Adventure Tour option for spelunkers. Each fall, there's even a nudist version of the cave tour. Howe also has an adventure park, gemstone mining, a restaurant, a sweet shop, and a gift store.

6 Lockport Cave and Underground Boat Ride

5 Gooding St., Lockport, NY 14094; 716-438-0174
www.lockportcave.com

Take a 70-minute guided tour about the "Flight of Five," aka Locks 67–71—part of the Erie Canal, which connects Albany to Buffalo. Besides learning about Lockport's industrial past, you'll see a cave full of geological formations and artifacts abandoned by the people

who built the 2,100-foot tunnel, blasted from solid rock in the 19th century to provide waterpower. Part of the tour includes a 40-foot underground boat ride along the Erie Canal. Special fall lantern, Halloween, and ghost tours are available too. If that's not adventurous enough for you, try zip lining across the Erie Canal and back. Tours are seasonal.

7 Natural Stone Bridge and Caves

535 Stone Bridge Road, Pottersville, NY 12860; 518-494-2283
www.stonebridgeandcaves.com

Boasting the largest marble cave entrance in the eastern United States, this 0.75-mile, self-guided, aboveground nature trail leads past the old Sawmill Site Waterfalls, the Artists' Gorge, some potholes, grottoes, and surface caves. There are plenty of benches where you can rest along the way. There's also an Adventure Tour that has you don special gear before crawling through sand, mud, rock, and an underground waterfall before floating through Garnet Cave. In the winter, 14.5 miles of trails are accessible via snowshoes. If you don't feel like hiking, there's a playground, snack bar, picnic areas, several family-friendly activities, and the PBS video *Under the Adirondacks,* which plays on loop by the gift store.

8 Secret Caverns

671 Caverns Road, Howes Cave, NY 12092; 518-296-8558
www.secretcaverns.com

Walk down 103 damp stone steps and navigate twists and turns to see a 100-foot underground waterfall. Wear sturdy boots and old clothes—you might get muddy! A chatty guide makes jokes and tells you about how two cows allegedly found the cave, open to sightseers since 1929, and stories about the different rock formations. He'll turn lights on and off as you go and allow the cave to go completely dark at one point—an unnerving experience. The funky store displays fluorescent–painted signs and pictures on its walls. The same artist who did them also designed the cups and T-shirts sold in the gift shop. There's a covered area with picnic tables and an ice cave that you can visit.

Howe Passageway

A vintage locomotive at the Delaware & Ulster Railroad Depot

FALL LEAF-PEEPING season begins in late September and lasts through October, although color changes depend on elevation, weather, and temperature. While the Adirondacks and Catskills especially color the mountains with rich reds, ambers, and oranges, all of New York State offers vibrant views. Come November, it's time to think about Santa Claus and the perennial tale of the Polar Express. Train tours sell out quickly, so make your reservations early.

SEASONAL ACTIVITIES

1 Adirondack Scenic Railroad, *Utica and Thendara Stations* *120*
This historic railroad goes to several destinations. If you're in the holiday mood,
there are Haunted History Evenings, the Polar Express, and more.

2 Arcade & Attica Railroad, *Arcade.* *120*
Board vintage trains to visit a historic depot, say hello to Santa, or enjoy the
beauty of fall's leaves—plus theme tours.

3 Catskill Mountain Railroad, *Kingston.* *121*
The popular Polar Express tickets go on sale in June. The railroad also offers
holiday tours for Halloween and Easter.

4 Delaware & Ulster Railroad's Silver Sleigh, *Arkville.* *121*
Hear the legend of how a steamliner rescued Old St. Nick one snowy Christmas
Eve as you eat cookies and drink hot cocoa.

1 Adirondack Scenic Railroad

Utica Station, 321 Main St., Utica, NY 13501; 800-819-2291
Thendara Station, 2568 NY 28, Thendara, NY 13472; 800-819-2291
www.adirondackrr.com

Celebrate the seasons with a train ride—see the fall foliage, enjoy time with Santa Claus, watch the *Polar Express* become real, and more. You'll board a vintage train, which chugs over historic tracks—restored by the Adirondack Railway Preservation Society—as the scenic Adirondacks pass by. Some tours have general seating while others, such as the 2-hour Polar Express, offer "Cocoa Class," aka first class (table seating and service, hot cocoa, and cookies), and coach. You can also bring food and beverages if you like, but not alcohol. Tours go rain or shine and are round-trip, except for the Bike & Rail trip, in which you pedal back. Other fun trains to choose from have beer and wine and princess/superhero themes.

2 Arcade & Attica Railroad

278 Main St., Arcade, NY 14009; 585-492-3100
www.aarailroad.com

Vintage trains can take you to see the fall foliage (weekends in October) and Curriers Station, an antique train depot, or you can board the North Pole Express and visit with Santa Claus at his house, where kids get a gift, toy, and bell and do all sorts of festive holiday activities (November and December). There are lots of fun theme tours to choose from, too, like A&A's murder-mystery train with dinner served during the "intermission"; Civil War Week, with demos and reenactors; or the Great Train Robbery, where you go back in time to the Wild West. Rides last from 90 minutes to about 2.5 hours, depending on the tour you select. Leave yourself time to enjoy the historic station, which features exhibits and fun antiques like old railroad lanterns.

3 Catskill Mountain Railroad

Westbrook Lane Station, Kingston Plaza, 55 Plaza Road, Kingston, NY 12401;
845-332-4854
www.catskillmountainrailroad.com

The Polar Express is so popular that tickets go on sale in June. This version stays true to the classic story of a boy's adventure in the North Pole. Your "golden ticket" gets punched, hot chocolate and cookies are handed out, the book by Chris Van Allsburg is read, and carols are sung. At the North Pole, Santa and friends come aboard, hand out silver bells, and pose for pictures. Peak and off-peak ticket prices are available (determined on the date you choose), and you'll save $1 per ticket if you book online. Other tours include the Catskill Fall Flyer (in September and October), perfect for leaf peeping; the Halloween-oriented Pumpkin Express and Rails of Terror; and the Easter Bunny Express, where you hunt for eggs and meet the most famous rabbit around.

4 Delaware & Ulster Railroad's Silver Sleigh

43510 NY 28, Arkville, NY 12406; 800-225-4132
www.durr.org

Listen to the story of how the classic vintage steamliner you're riding helped Santa Claus on a snowy Christmas Eve, with a photo-op visit with the big man himself. Homemade cookies, hot cocoa, and the winter landscape passing by your window make the ride festive (runs November and December). Other tours include the Pumpkin Patch Flyer (costumed kids accompanied by an adult and two food-pantry donations ride free) and a Rip Van Winkle Flyer, which offers lunch or dinner with reservations in a dining car. Located in the West Catskills, the train runs in the summer and fall and during some holidays. The D&U started in 1866 and was a Class 1 railroad often advertised as "the Only All-Rail Route to the Catskill Mountains."

Belleayre Mountain Ski Resort

WITH MORE THAN 50 ski resorts in New York, opportunities to ski, tube, snowboard, and enjoy other winter sports abound. These sites each offer something unique, including an association with the Olympics (Whiteface Mountain) and an 18-hole disc golf course you can play for free (Hunter Mountain). Enjoy winter recreation when it's cold, and then come back as the weather warms for adventure parks, hiking, and other fun in the sun.

SKIING

1 Belleayre Mountain Ski Area

181 Galli Curci Road, Highmount, NY 12441; 800-942-6904
www.belleayre.com

Less crowded than some resorts, this state-run mountain offers something for everyone with 51 trails, five glades, eight lifts, and 175 skiable acres. With a variety of beginner trails segregated from the rest of the mountain, newbies can find their ski legs before tackling tougher spaces with veterans. Boarders can expect two progression parks full of jumps, boxes, and rails. Cross-country skiers and snowshoers will enjoy almost 6 miles of quiet trails. The summit is just over 3,400 feet, and the vertical drop is 1,400 feet. There is lots of après-ski activity, with four lodges—two with cafeterias, lounges, shops, and first aid stations. There are no on-site accommodations, but the ski center offers Ski and Stay packages, partnering with local properties (see website for details). Open year-round, Belleayre Mountain also offers hiking, biking, a beach, and scenic gondola rides during warmer months.

2 Holiday Valley

6557 Holiday Valley Road, Ellicottville, NY 14731; 716-699-2345
www.holidayvalley.com

Despite the small-town vibe, Holiday Valley offers many options: skiing, cross-country, tubing, showshoeing, an 18-hole double-black-diamond golf course, and an adventure park. On the 290 skiable acres, you'll find a modest 750-foot vertical drop and 60 trails. Try the fun Sky Flyer Mountain Coaster, where you ride in a car, alone or with a friend; you use levers for speed control as you zigzag down the mountain. Check the activities and events section on the website—Holiday Valley holds all types of interesting festivals, mudslides, and even pond skimming, where skiers and snowboarders attempt to glide across an ice-water-filled pond. Summer pastimes include mountain, road, and e-biking (an electric kick helps you pedal); golf; pools; and water sports at Spruce Lake. Two on-site properties offer lodging.

3 Hunter Mountain

64 Klein Ave., Hunter, NY 12442; 800-486-8376
www.huntermtn.com

With 320 skiable acres—three mountains—in the Northern Catskills, the terrain provides beautiful scenery and opportunities for all levels of skiers. You'll find lots of fun all year long. Just look at the numbers: 67 trails, 13 lifts, four freestyle areas, and a 1,600-foot vertical drop. In the winter, there's skiing, snow tubing, ice climbing and rappelling, and snowcat tours. When the snow melts, the adventure begins with several zip lining choices and a 60-foot-high tower with nine obstacles to navigate. There's also fly-fishing, hiking, 4x4 off-road tours, and a scenic sky ride to the 3,200-foot summit of Hunter Mountain. You can play the challenging 18-hole disc golf course for free, but you'll need to bring your own disc or buy one from the pro shop. Accommodations options include a lodge and condos.

4 Whiteface Mountain

5021 NY 86, Wilmington, NY 12997; 518-946-2223
www.whiteface.com

You'll find some novel experiences in Lake Placid: the 2.1-mile Wilmington Trail has the longest single intermediate run in the Northeast, according to the ski center website; you can bobsled down an Olympic track; and there's a crazy vertical drop of 3,430 feet—the largest one in the East. The 22-mile space contains three peaks and 86 trails lined with evergreens covered in snow. The 288 skiable acres includes 53 acres of glades skiing and 35 acres of in-bounds, off-piste, double-black-diamond wilderness terrain (conditions permitting). The fifth-highest mountain in New York State offers stunning views of the Adirondacks and Lake Champlain. Other activities include gondola rides, driving tours along the scenic Veterans' Memorial Highway, biking, and more. Dining options are available, from café to bar/grill fare. Whitehouse also holds events and competitions (check website for details).

Skiing

Rockland Center for the Arts

NEW YORK CITY isn't the only place to find good theater and art. Throughout the state, summer theaters produce opera, musicals, plays, and events worthy of Lincoln Center or the Great White Way. There are places to see art and sculpture—and not just in museums, but also on nature trails and alongside a canal.

THE ARTS

1 Bethel Woods Center for the Arts

200 Hurd Road, Bethel, NY 12720; 866-781-2922
www.bethelwoodscenter.org

The site of the 1969 Woodstock Festival still celebrates performance, with Bethel's events, programs, lectures, and discussions. Their facilities house a large outdoor amphitheater that can hold 15,000 people, an indoor event gallery for 440, a conservatory used for educational programs, and a museum that places a special emphasis on Woodstock's history. The 800-acre center is known for its festivals, including an annual Harvest and Wine fete, as well as a Holiday Market. The nonprofit offers programs for all ages, including outdoor movies, book launches, screenings, classes, and free family fun days like its Halloween in the Woods. Some events do sell out, so plan accordingly. The Bindy Bazaar Museum Store sells souvenirs with a 1960s flavor.

2 Forestburgh Playhouse

39 Forestburgh Road, Forestburgh, NY 12777; 845-794-1194
www.fbplayhouse.org

The playhouse runs musicals and plays on its main stage, along with youth theater productions and cabaret performances with dinner at the adjoining Forestburgh Tavern. The playhouse, the oldest continuously operating summer theater in New York State, also offers educational opportunities. Initially a repurposed barn, the cozy 270-seat theater opened in 1947 with a production of *Blithe Spirit*. Now they've done more than 250 shows. You'll find some of Broadway's best hits at the playhouse, such as *Venus in Fur, Hair,* and *The Producers,* from mid-June to Labor Day. The tavern offers a cabaret with buffet prior to the main show, as well as after-theater weekend shows with cocktails and food. A Fall Series runs Friday and Saturday nights, September–Columbus Day.

3 Frank J. Ludovico Sculpture Trail

77 Bridge St., Seneca Falls, NY 13148; 315-568-8204
www.senecafalls.com/visit-seneca-falls.php

The woodsy, 1-mile-plus trail features sculptures, benches, and picturesque bridges—making it an easy and enjoyable walk alongside the south shore of the Cayuga-Seneca Canal. Local and national female artists predominantly created the sculptures inspired by the women's movement, Seneca Falls, and the canal. Located near the Women's Rights National Historic Park (see page 106), the sculpture trail opened in 1999 and is named after the man who donated its land. The converted railway bed is appropriate for hikers, dog walkers, bicyclers, and cross-country skiers. It will eventually be part of the Erie Canalway Trail.

4 The Glimmerglass Festival

Box office: 18 Chestnut St., Cooperstown, NY 13326; 607-547-2255
www.glimmerglass.org

The yearly festival, held at the 918-seat Alice Busch Opera Theater on Otsego Lake, produces four works each summer (three operas and a musical) as well as other performances like cabarets, concerts, and lectures. The open-air theater uses sliding walls that allow air in before performances and at intermission—a lovely effect, but one without climate control, so dress accordingly. Take advantage of the festival's previews, with an expert offering insights on the opera that you'll see an hour before showtime. Sessions are free for ticket holders. Come early so you can wander the grounds with its rolling hills. There is plenty of picnic space for al fresco dining. You can also purchase tickets for backstage tours (see schedule online).

5 Rockland Center for the Arts (RoCA)

27 S. Greenbush Road, West Nyack, NY 10994; 845-358-0877
www.rocklandartcenter.org

RoCA has quite the pedigree—its founders include composers Aaron Copland and Kurt Weill and actress Helen Hayes, who wanted to support arts and culture outside of New York City. The center, started in 1947, keeps that original agenda, seeking to create and promote art through a variety of events, exhibitions, and educational opportunities. An ever-evolving sculpture park surrounds the facility and places outdoor art on its trails that connect to Palisades Park. It's open daily until dusk, and it's free! Inside you can see contemporary art exhibits and catch workshops and events. The school offers all types of classes, from ceramics to creative writing to fine arts in state-of-the-art studios for all levels, including weekend and family workshops.

Brotherhood Winery

FINDING GOOD VINO isn't difficult in New York State, especially with all of the wine trails available. Spend the day touring the wineries, and you'll see beautiful lakes, farmlands, vineyards, and forests while you enjoy sampling the wares. These sites offer more than grape-oriented beverages, however: there are also distilleries and cideries on many of the trails. Often locations offer food, events, and live music—making it fun even if you don't imbibe.

WINE TRAILS

1 Dutchess Wine Trail

Clinton: 450 Schultzville Road, Clinton Corners, NY 12514; 845-266-5372
Millbrook: 26 Wing Road, Millbrook, NY 12545; 800-662-WINE
www.clintonvineyards.com, www.millbrookwine.com

Clinton Vineyards and the **Millbrook Vineyard & Winery**—within a 15-minute drive from each other—make up this trail that goes past orchards, farms, and forests in the Hudson Valley. The 100-acre Clinton specializes in the hardy Seyval Blanc grape, and its tasting area and gift shop are located in a charming 19th-century barn. Several tasting packages are available, including one with owner Phyllis Feder. Millbrook provides tours and tastings held in their 1940s Dutch-style barn. Varieties include Chardonnay, Cabernet Franc, and Riesling. There's also a tented café and picnic tables. The winery also offers Pinot Noir and wine-blending seminars and runs events like Jazz at the Grille and Friday Night Food Trucks.

2 Finger Lakes Wine Trails

Cayuga Lake, Keuka Lake, and Seneca Lake Wine Trails; 800-813-2958
www.fingerlakeswinecountry.com/wine-food/wine-trails

The Finger Lakes region offers three different wine trails for your sampling pleasure. The wineries host events such as food and wine pairings and live music. Look into the passport program for tasting discounts. Cayuga Lake is considered America's first wine trail and includes distilleries and cideries (see www.cayugawinetrail.com). Keuka Lake has a five-winery circuit that's easy to do in one day (see www.keukawinetrail.com). The Seneca Lakes Wine Trail features more than 30 wineries. You're sure to find the perfect wine while sampling through its 4,000-plus-mile trail (see www.senecalakewine.com/the-trail). Finally, the Finger Lakes Beer Trail (see www.fingerlakesbeertrail.com) is in this area, too, for all you craft beer fans.

3 Good Taste Artisanal Beverage Trail

Sullivan County, Catskills; 800-882-2287
www.sullivancatskills.com

Whether you're a beer, wine, cider, or spirits drinker, this wine trail, which winds through the Catskills and visits about a dozen stops, has something for every palate. Try some organic lavender wine and farm-to-table Mexican and South American food at **Bashakill Vineyards,** or maybe cider made from heirloom apples and pears at **Seminary Hill,** harvested from their 60-acre orchard. You'll find a large outdoor beer garden at the **Roscoe Beer Company,** where you can eat, drink, and listen to live music. The **Callicoon Brewing Company** is housed in a converted firehouse that overlooks the Delaware River and serves craft brews. Like harder stuff? Go see how **Rock Valley Spirits** makes their products. For a trail map, check the website.

4 Lake Ontario Wine Trail

Finger Lakes; 800-527-6510
www.lakeontariowinetrail.com

This tour takes you from locations on Lake Ontario to cider mills and farms, and covers about eight wineries, cideries, and distilleries—**Colloca Estate Winery** (situated on a 103-acre waterfront estate), **Embark Craft Ciderworks** (a family farm since 1909), **JD Wine Cellars, Old Goat Cidery, Rootstock Cider & Spirits** (try their vodka made from apples), **Young Sommer Winery** (their outdoor patio is perfect for picnics), **Thorpe Vineyard** (owner Fumie Thorpe hosts events based on her meterology and astronomy background; see www.thorpevineyard.com for more details), and **Casa Larga Vineyards.** Check out the wine trail's events, such as its Christmas Around the World weekend, with international food and drink pairings, and the passport program, which can save you money on tastings.

5 Niagara Wine Trail

Greater Niagara region
www.niagarawinetrail.org

Explore the countryside of Niagara, Orleans, and Monroe Counties on this wine trail. The moderate climate in this area creates a growing season with long days, producing aromatic fruit that's full of flavor. The approximately 20 wineries on the trail feature vinifera varieties, such as Riesling, Pinot Gris, and Vidal Blanc, along with fruit wines, meads, and ciders. Vino Visa Passports, which contain coupons for the wineries, transportation, local restaurants, and lodging, are available for purchase. Some of the wineries offer food (**Honeymoon Trail Winery** does cheese pairings, for instance), some have spirits of the spooky, not drinkable, kind (the **Winery at Marjim Manor** tells ghost stories during your visit); and others are located on farms (**Vizcarra Vineyards,** for example, also has a market for homemade baked goods, jam and fudge, and in-season produce).

6 Shawangunk Wine Trail

Ulster and Orange Counties; 845-256-8456
www.shawangunkwinetrail.com

Visit some 15 wineries around the Shawangunk Mountains, about 60 miles from New York City. All of the family-owned sites on this 80-mile trail have unique attributes—some are famous, like **Brotherhood,** America's oldest winery, in Washingtonville, where you visit their underground cellars. There's lots of variety, from vinifera varietals to sparkling wines to hard ciders, distilled spirits, and even mead. The passport program allows you a wine tasting at each location at a fraction of the usual price. Check out the events calendar, too, for programs such as Wreath Fineries at the Wineries, in which you can shop, sample, and build a holiday wreath as you receive an ornament from each decorated winery. Various transportation services are available (see website for suggested list).

7 The Thousand Islands–Seaway Wine Trail

Thousand Islands
www.iloveny.com/listing/1000-islands-seaway-wine-trail/14254/

This 78-mile scenic drive showcases eight family-owned wineries and vineyards. Cold winters prevented this region from growing grapes until the University of Minnesota introduced a cold-hardy variety in 1966. Their locations include **Coyote Moon on the River, Northern Flow Vineyards** (located in DeLuke's Garden Center, they offer Plant and Sip nights; see www.northernflowvineyards.com), The **Cape Winery, Otter Creek Winery** (which produces over 7,000 gallons of more than 13 wine varieties), **White Caps Winery** (accessible by land and water, through the Chaumont Bay), **Thousand Islands Winery** (check out their family-friendly events at www.thousandislandswinery.com), **Venditti Vineyards,** and **Busted Grapes.** The wine trail's passport program, which is available at all sites, offers discounts at the wineries and partner businesses.

Stacked wine barrels in front of vineyard in Hudson Valley, upstate New York

Cloves of garlic at the Hudson Valley Garlic Festival

YOUR IDEAL DAY TRIP might involve sleuthing for antiques at a flea market or a quaint roadside shop, living it up at a wine festival, or maybe an old-fashioned day at a ballgame. Well, in any case, New York has you covered. Here are some of its best antiquing spots, festivals, and sporting venues, more than enough to keep you busy.

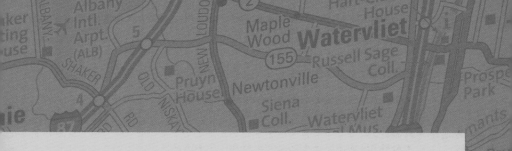

OTHER DAY TRIPS

Antiquing and Flea Markets

Adirondack Mountains Antiques Show (September)
Various locations along NY 28, Indian Lake, NY 12847; 518-648-5112
www.adirondackexperience.com/indian-lake/adirondack-mountains-antiques-show

Antique World (year-round)
11111 Main St., Clarence, NY 14031; 716-759-8483
www.antiqueworldmarket.com

Charlotte Flea Market (year-round)
4419–4421 Lake Ave., Rochester, NY 14612; 585-429-0675
www.charlottefleamarkets.com

City Market (second Sunday of the month, May–October)
Outside of the Everson Museum, 401 Harrison St., Syracuse, NY 13202; 315-481-9960
www.citymarketsyracuse.com

East Aurora Auction & Expo Center (year-round)
11167 Big Tree Road, East Aurora, NY 14052; 716-655-7500
www.eastauroraevents.com

East Avon Flea Market (Sundays April–May)
Henrietta Road, Avon, NY 14414; 585-226-8320
www.eastavonfleamarket.com

Madison-Bouckville Antique Week (August)
NY 20, Bouckville, NY 13310; 800-684-7320
www.madison-bouckville.com

Mower's Flea Market (weekends May–November)
11 Maple Lane, Woodstock, NY 12498; 845-679-6744
www.mowerssaturdayfleamarket.com

The Peddler Flea Market (Saturdays April–October)
656 Elmwood Ave., Buffalo 14222
www.facebook.com/pg/thepeddlerbuffalony

Stormville Airport Antique Show and Flea Market (six shows a year)
428 NY 216, Stormville, NY 12582; 845-221-6561
www.stormvilleairportfleamarket.com

Festivals and Fairs

Other
Day Trips

Catskill International Film Festival (August)
30 Upper Main St., Callicoon, NY 12723; 845-423-8845
www.filmfreeway.com/catskillinternationalfilmfestival

Catskills Wine and Food Festival (October)
Echo Campground, 210 Echo Road, Bloomingburg, NY 12721; 845-746-2270
www.catskillsfestival.com

Finger Lakes Musical Theatre Festival (May–October)
6877 East Lake Road, Auburn, NY 13021; 315-255-1785
www.fingerlakesmtf.com

The Great New York State Fair (summer)
581 State Fair Blvd., Syracuse, NY 13209; 800-475-FAIR
nysfair.ny.gov

Hudson Valley Garlic Festival (September)
Cantine Field, Washington Avenue Extension, Saugerties, NY 12477; 845-246-3090
www.hvgf.org

New York Renaissance Faire
(weekends August–October, Labor Day)
600 NY 17A, Tuxedo, NY 10987; 845-351-5171
www.renfair.com

Woodstock Film Festival (October)
13 Rock City Road, Woodstock, NY 12498; 845-679-4265
www.woodstockfilmfestival.org

Sports

Catskill Fly Fishing Center & Museum
1031 Old Route 17, Livingston Manor, NY 12758; 845-439-4810
www.cffcm.com

HITS (Hunter/Jumper Horse Shows)
454 Washington Ave. Extension, Saugerties, NY 12477; 845-246-5515
The Great New York State Fairgrounds, 581 State Fair Blvd., Syracuse, NY 13209;
315-487-7711
www.hitsshows.com

National Baseball Hall of Fame
25 Main St., Cooperstown, NY 13326; 888-HALL-OF-FAME
www.baseballhall.org

Olympic Sports Complex
220 Bobsled Run Road, Lake Placid, NY 12946; 518-523-4436
www.whiteface.com/facilities/olympic-sports-complex

Saratoga Race Course
267 Union Ave., Saratoga Springs, NY 12866; 844-NYRA-TIX
www.saratogaracetrack.com

A racehorse at Saratoga Springs

Roses

NEW YORK STATE
Symbols, Emblems, and Trivia

COUNTIES: 62
POPULATION, PER THE U.S. CENSUS: 19,542,209
(approximately 40 percent live in New York City)
FOUNDING AS U.S. STATE: July 9, 1776

STATE FLAG

New York's state flag includes nods to the Hudson River, the ships that have been plied the state's waters for hundreds of years, and it also includes the state motto, *Excelsior*, Latin for "ever upward." If you look closely, you'll also see a crown underneath the feet of Liberty; that's a reference to New York's central role in the Revolutionary War.

STATE FRUIT—Apple

Apples are New York's state fruit, and for good reason. New York produces more apples than almost any other state—only Washington State produces more. In a given year, New York produces more than 1 billion pounds of apples, enough for 50 pounds for all 19,542,209 New Yorkers.

STATE BIRD—Eastern Bluebird *(Sialia sialis)*

A beloved sign of spring, the bluebird was once in danger of extinction. Bluebirds nest in established cavities (holes) in trees; due to habitat loss and competition from introduced bird species for nest sites, bluebird populations once plummeted. Happily, people stepped in to help, providing artificial nest boxes—and new populations have thrived. To build your own, visit the New York State Bluebird Society for information (http://nysbs.org/).

STATE FLOWER—
Rose *(Rosa* spp.*)*

Whether it's an heirloom rose, a showy modern cultivar, or a wild rose tucked in a thicket, everyone loves this flower. New York has been a hotbed for rose gardens since the earliest days of settlement. There are rose gardens scattered across the state, and it's also home to historic rose varieties that date back—at times—to the state's early history.

STATE TREE—
Sugar Maple
(Acer saccharum)

While the likes of Quebec and Vermont are arguably more famous for their maple syrup, New York has more maple trees than any state and produces several hundred thousand gallons of maple syrup a year. It takes around 40 gallons of sap to produce a gallon of sugar, so you do the math—that's more than a few trees.

STATE BEVERAGE—Milk

You might not think of dairy farming when it comes to New York, but the state is the country's fifth largest producer. It's home to thousands of dairy farms, and the milk its cows produce is used in yogurt, cottage cheese, butter, and ice cream. Dairy brands based in New York or with New York ties include Chobani and Dannon.

STATE ANIMAL—North American Beaver *(Castor canadensis)*

Perhaps more than any other animal, the beaver has played an out-sized role in New York history. Famous for its sharp teeth and its strong tail, the beaver meant something else to early settlers in New York: money. Beaver pelts were widely traded and used to create high-end clothing, such as coats and hats. The trade in beaver pelts profoundly affected the state and its indigenous inhabitants, and it eventually led to the extirpation of the beaver altogether in some places, including New York City. Until recently, that is, beaver populations were reintroduced in upstate New York, and populations have recovered. In recent years, individual beavers have even been spotted in New York City itself.

STATE INSECT—Ladybug *(Coccinella novemnotata)*

For a time, New York's state insect, the nine-spotted ladybug, was feared extinct. Nine-spotted Ladybug populations vanished in the early 1980s. After decades of dedicated work from teams of scientists (not to mention plenty of citizen science volunteers filing field reports), much more is known about these still-struggling populations. To contribute your own observations, visit the Lost Ladybug Project's website (www.lostladybug.org)

STATE FRESHWATER FISH—Brook Trout
(Salvelinus fontanalis)

Once found throughout much of the state, the Brook Trout is now something of a rarity, found largely in ponds and streams of the Adirondacks. With populations severely impacted by acid rain, introduction of competing species, and declines in the insects it eats, the Brook Trout's population has declined across much of its former range. Nonetheless, it's still a popular target for anglers, thanks to its fine taste, and the sheer fun of catching a fish in one of the hundreds of brook trout ponds found in the Adirondacks.

STATE MARINE OR SALTWATER FISH— Striped Bass *(Morone saxatilis)*

Prized by both chefs and recreational anglers, the Striped Bass is a striking, gorgeous fish that can reach up to 4 feet in length. The fish, which can live for decades, have long been a commercial target for anglers, but over the past several decades, populations and harvests have plummeted due to overfishing and pollution concerns. As a result, Striped Bass rules and regulations have been in perennial flux in New York (and on the East Coast, generally), as regulators try to hone the best approach to protect these iconic fish.

STATE FOSSIL— Eurypterus Remipes

You won't find anything like this living in New York today— or anywhere. Denizens of an ancient sea some 400 million years ago, the genus Eurypterus are often known as "sea scorpions." Despite their fearsome name, they weren't actually scorpions, instead probably being most closely related to insects, crustaceans, and other wiggly kin. Most Eurypterids were quite small, but New York's state fossil (*E. remipes*) was huge, almost the size of a person.

STATE GEM—Garnet

Garnet is a hard, dark-red mineral that is a popular gemstone and also prized for its hardness. Because of its hardness, it's been used as an industrial abrasive for more than a century, and it has been an ingredient in select sandpapers, glass, and more. Garnet is found mostly in the Adirondack region, and there you can even find your own in some locations (for example: www.garnetminetours.com).

STATE BUSH—Lilac *(Syringa spp.)*

Native to Asia and parts of south-
ern Europe, lilacs are a common
sight around many parts of New York
state. Lilacs are especially popular in
Rochester, which has held
a lilac festival since 1898
and is home to hundreds
of different lilac varieties. The 10-day festival
includes a parade, a road
race, food, and more.

STATE REPTILE—Snapping Turtle *(Chelydra serpentina)*

Famously cantankerous, the snapping turtle is a common sight
around roadways (please don't hit them!), near wetlands, and in
New York lakes. These turtles can get pretty big—around 30 pounds
or so—and while they do have a powerful bite, you can avoid it by
simply staying away from them. Snapping turtles are found throughout much of New York, even in urban areas such as Central Park.

STATE SNACK—Yogurt

Given how much milk the state produces, it shouldn't be a surprise that New York also makes a lot of other dairy products, especially yogurt. In fact, New York was at the center of the Greek yogurt craze, which has since become a US dietary staple.

STATE SHELL—Bay Scallop *(Argopecten irradians)*

Long a popular seafood, the Bay Scallop's populations have suffered in recent years due to habitat loss, pollution, and other threats. Populations are still down, compared to historic totals, but limited recreational collecting of bay scallops is now allowed. As an organism, the bay scallop is fascinating—it has more than a dozen sets of eyes (which are blue, no less), and its empty shells are a common beach find on much of the East Coast.

STATE MUFFIN—Apple Muffin

An official state muffin might sound odd—only two other states have one—but the backstory is adorable: In the 1980s, elementary school students in New York lobbied legislators to create an official state muffin, and they even ended up providing a recipe. If you want to try it for yourself, search for it here: https://www.applesfromny.com

Apple Muffin

Index

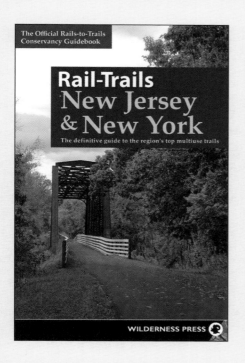

Check out this great title from **WILDERNESS PRESS!**

Rail-Trails New Jersey & New York

Rails-to-Trails Conservancy

ISBN: 978-0-89997-965-6 • $18.95 • 5.5 x 8.5 • paperback
232 pages • full-color maps and photos

The Official Rails-to-Trails Conservancy Guidebook

All across the country, unused railroad corridors have been converted into public multiuse trails. Here, the experts from Rails-to-Trails Conservancy present the best of these rail-trails, as well as other multiuse pathways, in New Jersey and New York. You'll appreciate the detailed maps for each trail, plus driving directions to trailheads. Quick, at-a-glance icons indicate which activities each trail can accommodate, from biking to fishing to snowmobiling. Explore 58 of the best rail-trails and multiuse pathways across two states.

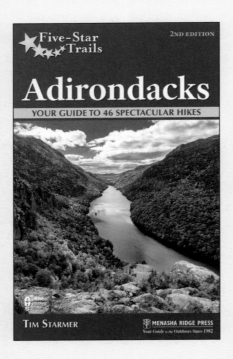

Five-Star Trails: Adirondacks

Tim Starmer

ISBN: 978-1-63404-052-5 • $16.95 •
2nd edition • 5 x 8 • paperback • 304 pages

Find the Top Trails in This Famous Region!

The Adirondack Park is an immense wilderness, encompassing more than 9,375 square miles. Within its boundaries are rugged mountains, countless pristine lakes and ponds, seemingly endless forests, and thousands of miles of wild rivers. *Five-Star Trails: Adirondacks* is your detailed guide to some of the most stunning views in New York. Each trail entry has been thoroughly researched and features a trail map, elevation profile, and key at-a-glance information.